MORE PRAISE FOR *Approaching the Qur'an*

"When a ranking Islamicist brings to his translation a mastery of English language that equals that of the best poets of our day, the result is certain to be remarkable. And, as here demonstrated, it is. After Michael Sells' breakthrough rendition of the Qur'an's earliest chapters, the English-speaking world need never again find that holy text impenetrable."

> HUSTON SMITH is author of the bestselling work *The World's Religions* and *Why Religion Matters*.

"*Approaching the Qur'an* is a sensitive and unusually accessible first book on the Qur'an and its function as scripture for over one-seventh of the human race. This book opens up many facets of the special role that the Qur'an plays in Muslim life and thought. Dr. Sells is to be congratulated for a significant contribution to English-language materials on the Qur'an."

> WILLIAM A. GRAHAM is professor of the History of Religion and Islamic Studies at Harvard University, and author of *Divine Word, Prophetic Word in Early Islam*.

"Michael Sells' *Approaching the Qur'an* is much more than a translation of the Qur'an. The work is a carefully considered introduction to a religious appreciation of the text from within a scholarly framework. By highlighting issues of the multiple levels upon which the text conveys its meaning to its readers and auditors, Sells manages to overcome the first impression that many people have of the Qur'an being a 'difficult' book. The structure of *Approaching the Qur'an*, with its parallel translation and commentary, will prove valuable both for interested general readers and for students studying the text within a classroom setting."

> ANDREW RIPPIN is professor of Islamic and Religious Studies, University of Calgary, associate editor of the *Encyclopedia of the Qur'an*, and editor of *Approaches to the History of the Interpretation of the Qur'an*.

"Despite the rapid growth of Islam in this century, its precepts and scripture remain inaccessible to many readers. This groundbreaking work goes a very long way to bridging the gap that separates the non-Islamic reader from the Qur'an. Highly recommended."

> *Library Journal*

Approaching

The

Qur'án

Approaching
The
Qur'án

The Early Revelations

INTRODUCED AND TRANSLATED

BY MICHAEL SELLS

WHITE CLOUD PRESS

ASHLAND, OREGON

First Edition: 1999
Second printing: 2001

Cover design: David Rupee, Impact Publications
Cover photograph by Laleh Bakhtiar
Photographs courtesy of Alharamain Foundation (pp.13, 32, 46, 70, 144, 182); Laleh Bakhtiar (pp. 77, 154); Jeff Zundel (pp. 102, 142, 169).
Type design: Dominion font created by Dr. Christopher Buck

LIBRARY OF CONGRESS CATALOGING IN PUBLICATION DATA
Koran. English.
    Approaching the Qur'an / introduced and translated by Michael Sells.
        p.   cm.
    ISBN 1-883991-30-7 (hardcover). -- 1-883991-26-9 (paperback)
    1. Koran--Criticism, interpretation, etc.   I. Sells, Michael Anthony.
        II. Title
    BP1091999
    297.1'2261--dc21   99-13401
                                                         CIP

02 03 04 05   10 9 8 7 6

Dedicated to the memory of Jeanette Wakin

Table of Contents

Acknowledgments   *viii*

Note on Transliteration   *ix*

Introduction: Approaching the Qur'an   1

Glossary of Arabic Terms   35

The Early Suras with Commentary   42

Hearing the Qur'an: 145
The Call to Prayer and Six Suras

Sound, Spirit and Gender in the Qur'an   183

Selected Further Resources   *208*

Compact Disc Selections of Qur'anic Recitation   *216*

Biographies of Qur'anic Reciters   *218*

Acknowledgments to:

Mahmoud Ayoub, Emil Homerin, Kristina Nelson, Anne Rasmussen, and Anna Margaret Gade for their expertise and counsel; Imam Zijad Delic, Imam Bilal Hyde, Amir Koushkani and Hajjah Maria Ulfa for their support of this project and the use of their recitations; Steven Zaban of Dream On Productions for his generosity in providing reasonable rates and studio types for the recording of Seemi Bushra Ghazi and Imam Zijad and for his editing of the Bilal Hyde Fatiha, Osman Samad for his recording of Bilal Hyde's recitation of the Fatiha at the wedding of Omid Safi to Holly Frigon on July 31, 1999; Students, colleagues, and administration of Haverford College for their encouragement throughout the fifteen years of work on this project and for the faculty research grants that helped support it; The National Endowment for the Humanities and the John Simon Guggenheim Foundation for support in the study of early Arabic literature; Ron Ditmars for his continuing commitment to the importance of the aural component of religious experience and revelation; Michael Haxby, Aida Premilovac, and Alan Smith for their readings of the manuscript and editorial suggestions; The students and faculty of Middle Eastern Studies at Columbia University, Emory University, and the University of Michigan for their hospitality and critical engagement with this material; The Middle East Studies Association and the American Academy of Religion, at the annual conferences of which material from this book was first presented.

Special thanks to Seemi Bushra Ghazi for corrections to the manuscript, advice on recording, help in arranging recording sessions, sensitivity to the Qur'an, and the wisdom, generosity, and spirit she has contributed to this project.

Note on Transliteration

In the prose commentaries and in the transliterations given underneath the translations, I have used the standard transliterations in which vowels that are held for a double duration are given a macron. Thus "ā" indicates a vowel that is double the length of "a". This quantitative system is similar to that of classical Greek and Latin, but does not translate directly into the English rhythms based upon a stress accent. Thus, in Arabic poetry and formal measure, the woman's name Laylā is pronounced with quantitively lengthened final "a". However, in much informal speech and especially when used in English, the word is pronounced Láyla, with a stress accent on the "ay".

It makes no sense, indeed it is counterproductive, to place indications of quantitative vowel length in translations where the verbal rhythm and measure is based upon stress. To the extent such markings would be understood, they would introduce a disruption in the English measure. Thus, throughout the translations, I have used only an acute accent to mark the stress, but have dispensed with formal transliterations. Elsewhere, I use the standard method of macrons for long vowels and dots under consonants that do not exist in English and have no clear parallel.

In areas where the rhythm is important, I use the transliterations to reflect the actual sound of the formal pronunciation, and thus, where a long vowel is elided to a short vowel when followed by certain sounds, I dispense with the macron: compare the first word in ʿalā khayri l-ʿamal (to the best work) to the same word in ʿala l-falāḥ (to prosperity).

With names that have now an accepted and widely known English equivalent, I have also dispensed with transliteration: Muhammad as opposed to Muḥammad.

Introduction

Approaching the Qur'án

O NE AFTERNOON IN CAIRO, I found my- self in an unusual situation. The streets of this noisy, bustling city were suddenly strangely quiet, yet the cafes were crowded with people clustered around televisions. For special events—the death of a great figure, an important soccer game—one might expect to find people in cafes following the event on television. What had drawn people from the streets into the cafes today was the appearance of one of Egypt's popular Qur'an reciters. When I returned to my hotel, the lobby was filled with men, some of them Egyptian Christians, watching and lis- tening to the televised recitation with intense interest.

Such appreciation for the recited Qur'an stimulates a diver- sity of explanations. To devout Muslims, the recited Qur'an is the word of God revealed to the prophet Muhammad; its divine origin accounts for its hold over the listener. Some anti-Islamic mission- aries attribute the extraordinary power and beauty of the Qur'an to a Jinni or even Satan. A Marxist revolutionary from an Islamic background, who was highly critical of all religion, insisted that the genius of the Qur'an resulted from Muhammad's alleged madness and resultant close contact with the unconscious. In Middle Eastern societies, what unites these opinions and seems beyond dispute is the fact that the recited Qur'an is a distinctively compelling example of verbal expression.

The Qur'an itself offers an explanation for its unusual effect on its audience. In seventh-century Arabia, a man named Muhammad began reciting what he said were revelations to him from God. These revelations referred to themselves as the Qur'an. They present Muhammad as a prophet in the line of prophets stretching back from Jesus to Moses and Abraham. The Qur'an recounts the stories of earlier prophets with descriptions of their miracles: the marvels of Moses before Pharoah and Jesus bringing dead creatures back to life, for example. When a listener challenged Muhammad to prove he was a prophet by performing a miracle, the Qur'anic answer was that the Qur'an itself was the miracle. If anyone could produce anything like it, then the Qur'an was a human creation and Muhammad a false prophet. If, however, no one else could produce anything like it, then the Qur'an was clearly beyond the capacity of a human being, and Muhammad was not its author but simply its messenger. Although poets and others have taken up the Qur'anic challenge, including the famous and beloved poet nicknamed al-Mutannabi (the "Would-Be Prophet"), within Islam the Qur'an has been generally recognized as inimitable.

Most of the world's Muslims, including the majority of those who live outside the Arab world, learn the Qur'an in Arabic. For them, the sense of some extraordinary power and beauty in its language is readily recognized. Generations of Qur'anic commentators have tried to account for the compelling nature of the composition, articulation, or voice of the Qur'an in Arabic, but the fact that there was something special about it was assumed. It was apparent from the love of people for the Qur'anic voice; from the intertwining of the Qur'anic allusions and rhythms in the rich fabric of art, literature, and music; from the way the Qur'an is recited at great occasions and in the most humble circumstances of daily life; and from the devotion people put into learning to recite it correctly in Arabic. The sound of Qur'anic recitation can move people to tears, from 'Umar, the powerful second Caliph of Islam, to the average farmer, villager, or townsman of today, including those who may not be particularly observant or religious in temperament.

Yet for Westerners who do not read or speak Arabic, the effort to get even a basic glimpse of what the Qur'an is about has proved frustrating. The Qur'an is not arranged in chronological order or narrative pattern. Indeed, the passages associated with the very first revelations given to Muhammad, those learned first by Muslims when they study the Qur'an in Arabic, are placed at the very end of the written Qur'an. After a short prayer, the written Qur'an begins with the longest and one of the most complex chapters, one from Muhammad's later career, which engages the full array of legal, historical, polemical, and religious issues in a fashion bewildering for the reader not immersed in the history and law of early Islam. For those familiar with the Bible, it would be as if the second page opened with a combination of the legal discussions in Leviticus, the historical polemic in the book of Judges, and apocalyptic allusions from Revelation, with the various topics mixed in together and beginning in mid-topic.

This volume is an attempt to approach the Qur'an in two senses. First, in the translations and commentary I have tried to bring across some sense of that particular combination of majesty and intimacy that makes the Qur'anic voice distinctive. Second, I have sought to allow the reader who is unfamiliar with the details of Islamic history to approach the Qur'an in a way that allows an appreciation of its distinctive literary character. The selections presented here are the short, hymnic chapters or *Sūras* associated with the first revelations to Muhammad, most of which appear at the end of the written text and are commonly reached only by the most resolute reader. These short Suras are the sections learned first by Muslims in their study of the Arabic Qur'an. They also comprise the verses most often memorized, quoted, and recited. They contain some of the most powerful prophetic and revelatory passages in religious history. And they offer the vision of a meaningful and just life that anchors the religion of one-fifth of the world's inhabitants.

These passages involve relatively little of the historical, political, and legal detail present in the Suras associated with Muhammad's later career, after he became the leader of a young Islamic state. In this sense they are the Suras that speak most directly to every human being, regardless of religious confession or cultural background. As opposed to the Suras of the later period with their distinctive long verses, these early Suras are characterized by a hymnic quality, condensed and powerful imagery, and a sweeping lyricism. Opposite each Sura in this volume, you will find a short commentary that explores some of its subtleties and context. An annotated index at the end of the introduction explains key Qur'anic concepts and gives the Arabic terms and the English translations used for them in this volume. The purpose of this introduction is to clarify the cultural and historical matrix in which the Qur'an came to exist, the central themes and qualities of the hymnic Suras, and the manner in which the Qur'an is experienced and taken to heart within Islamic societies.

Since the Qur'an first became known in medieval Europe, it has been involved in the struggle between Christian Europe and Islam that culminated in the crusades and continued through the period of colonial rule and beyond. In recent centuries Europeans and Americans commonly assumed that the Qur'an was composed or fabricated by Muhammad; they referred to Islam as "Muhammadanism." Muslims view the term "Muhammadan" as profoundly misleading; contemporary scholars point out that it is invalid, since it implies that Muslims worship Muhammad in the way Christians worship Christ. If there is any analogue to Christ in Islam, as the "word of God" and the guide to the just life, it is not Muhammad but the Qur'an itself.

In the past few decades, non-Muslim scholars of Islam have adopted a less polemical approach. The Suras are attributed, in a more theologically neutral fashion, to the Qur'an as a text, rather than to whomever the interpreter considered the true author. Such attributions, now also common for the Bible, allow for a text to be discussed without constant and tendentious assumptions about its authorship. Even so, scholarly controversies continue. Thus, while most scholars treat the Qur'an as a text that was revealed or created in the time of Muhammad, a revisionist school views it as an oral tradition that may have extended beyond the lifetime of any single individual.[1]

The purpose of this book is neither to refute nor to promote the Qur'anic message. Rather, the goal is to allow those who do not have access to the Qur'an in its recited, Arabic form to encounter one of the most influential texts in human history in a manner that is accessible. These Suras contain the essential world view of the Qur'an concerning the meaning of life and the possibility of justice—the two interconnected themes that are at the heart of Islamic thought. This volume is devoted to these early Qur'anic revelations.

I. Muhammad, the Qur'án, and the Poets

According to traditional accounts, Muhammad was born in the year 570 C.E. in the trading town of Mecca, situated in a barren valley in central Arabia. Muhammad's father died before his birth. His mother died soon after. His grandfather, who had been appointed his guardian, also died while Muhammad was still a boy. He then came under the guardianship of an uncle. The Qur'an suggests that Muhammad's consciousness was deeply influenced by his experience of being orphaned in a society in which status, security, and life itself depended upon family connections.

Muhammad married Khadija, a prosperous widow and independent businesswoman who, along with her husband, was to exercise an enormous impact on world history. Muhammad had also taken to meditating in a cave in the rocky hills above Mecca and, around the year 610 C.E., he experienced his prophetic vision and first revelation. The vision is described in elliptic and allusive language (Sura 53). The first auditory revelation is believed to have been the Qur'anic words (Sura 96): "Recite in the name of your lord who created . . . " The term *Qur'ān*, given to the revelations Muhammad would convey, is related to the Arabic word for "recite." It might be translated as the Recitation.

The Qur'anic revelations present Muhammad as the "messenger" *(rasūl)* of God, the culmination in a line going back through many prophets found also in the Bible (Jesus, Moses, and Abraham) and through others known only in the Arabian tradition. At first, Muhammad was dismissed with contempt and mockery. Gradually, however, he built a small circle of followers, including Khadija and his cousin 'Ali. The revelations believed to be the earliest were embraced by a small group of people in a region considered a no-man's land by the leaders of the great empires of the day (Roman, Persian, and Ethiopian). Within the span of a few decades, these revelations became the core of a major world religion and an international civilization extending from what is now Spain to Afghanistan; within a couple of centuries, that faith extended all the way to China.

When Muhammad began reciting the verses translated here, Arabia was a vast empty space on the geopolitical map, a region little known and of little concern to the three major civilizations that surrounded it. To the north and west was the Byzantine Roman empire; to the northeast the Sassanian Persian empire; and to the southeast the Abyssinian-Yemenite civilization. Each of these empires had satellite Arab tribes more or less under its political and cultural influence. Each had ancient Arab cities associated with it: the Nabataean cities of Petra in the North, the Yemenite civilizations of Sheba and the Ma'rib dam in the south, and the kingdom of al-Hira in what is now Iraq, which was the capital of the Persian-leaning Arab tribes.

In the center of this world, at the blank spot on the geopolitical map, were the bedouin. Over centuries they had developed a way of life adapted to the brutal conditions of the desert. The bedouin herded sheep and goats and developed sciences of horse and camel breeding. The sparsity of desert vegetation forced the tribes into continual migration and into a situation of negotiation, rivalry, and frequent warfare over valued pasture grounds. Yet, despite the physical impoverishment of bedouin life, the bedouin were viewed as the authentic bearers of culture. Even the townsmen of Mecca looked to the bedouin as the personification of Arab values (the word *'arab* originally meant a pastoral nomad), and Muhammad himself was sent out to live with the family of his wet nurse in order to be educated in bedouin cultural values.

At the time Muhammad was reciting the first Qur'anic revelations to a skeptical audience in the town of Mecca, several developments were leading to a transformation of Arabia's place in
the world. One was a technological revolution. Sometime around
the period of Muhammad's life, the bedouin developed a new
kind of camel saddle that allowed their camels to carry previously
unimagined weight. Camels, which had been used largely for
milk and transport of individuals and small loads, became the center of a transportation revolution. Within a hundred years, the
Hellenistic and Roman worlds of transport and commerce, based
on donkey carts and the upkeep of roads, were replaced by camel
caravans. And the bedouin in Arabia, who had been traders with
and raiders of the established civilizations, were to control the
vehicle of trade and commerce in the Western world: the drome-
dary camel.[2]

Parallel to the technological revolution was a cultural and linguistic transformation. Muhammad recited to an audience that
had developed one of the most finely honed and scrutinizing tastes
in the history of expressive speech. This love for language had been
associated with the prophetic utterances of pre-Islamic seers
(kāhins) and especially with the poets (shā'irs) of Arabia who had
developed, over unknown centuries of oral tradition, a poetic her-
itage that, along with the Qur'an, was to become the wellspring for
the new Arabic-Islamic civilizations. Indeed, when Muhammad
first began reciting verses of particular power and beauty, some
called him a poet. A Qur'anic revelation made a distinction: poets
speak out of desire and do not understand what they are saying,
while a prophet speaks what is revealed to him by God (Sura 26).

Every year, at pilgrimage sites around Arabia, tribes gathered
for religious observances, trade, and poetry contests. One of the
major sites was Mecca, with its ancient shrine, the Ka'ba, an
empty, square enclosure with a black rock embedded in one wall.
The pilgrimage rituals in Mecca included the circumambulation of
the Ka'ba (the ritual circling of the shrine), as well as the "stations"
of pilgrimage around the precinct of Mecca itself that made up
the larger ritual known as the ḥajj. As tribes came to Mecca dur-

7

ing the "sacred months," all warfare and blood feuds were forbidden. During this period trade fairs and poetry contests were held outside of Mecca in a place known as known as 'Ukāẓ. According to legend, the seven most admired poems were embroidered in gold on rare black cloth and suspended from the walls of the Ka'ba. These "Hanging Odes" (Mu'allaqāt) served as the epitome of pre-Islamic bedouin cultural values and verbal expression.

The poets, the bearers of the values, were the most dangerous and obdurate opponents of the prophet Muhammad. At some point Muhammad found a circle of poets to support him as well, and the ancient poetic tradition then became a central part of the struggle. One of the most important figures in the Arabia of Muhammad's time was the poet Ka'b bin Zuhayr. As the son of Zuhayr (author of one of the celebrated "Hanging Odes") and a great poet in his own right, Ka'b was viewed within bedouin society as a cultural authority. His opposition to Muhammad continued until it became clear that Muhammad's political and cultural authority could no longer be challenged. By the standards of tribal code, as the spokesman for the losing side, Ka'b was in grave danger. In a famous episode, Ka'b went to the prophet Muhammad, offered his allegiance, and presented a poem in honor of the prophet. Muhammad then gave Ka'b his mantle (burda), and the poem has since been known as the burda or Mantle Ode. This transaction, as much as anything in early Islamic history, symbolizes the passing of the old order, the rejection of some of its values, and the transformation of other values into the new Islamic world-view. Even so, the tradition begun with pre-Islamic poetry continued to develop through the history of Arabic literature, even as it played an important role within Persian, Ottoman Turkish, Urdu, and the other literatures of Islam.

The odes (qasīdas) were constructed with three major sections: the remembrance of the lost beloved, the quest, and the boast. This poetry was heroic in values, lyrical in form, and dramatic in idiom. Remembrance of the beloved was based upon the broken relationship between lovers and beloveds. Love affairs begun when the bedouin tribes met at the fairs would be broken off as the tribes separated to pursue the year-long effort to find pasture grounds.

The abandoned ruins of the beloved's campsite became the quintessential symbol of the former union with the beloved and her current absence, and the generative symbol for the entire poem. The poet might also remember the stations of the beloved's journey away from him, and list them with ritual solemnity, as if they were the stations of a pilgrimage. The memory of the beloved, finally, would lead to a reverie, with a lyrical evocation of spring, of the oasis, of animals at peace—in other words, of a lost garden symbolic of the lost beloved.

The quest or "night journey" began when the poet broke out of his reverie and set off alone across the desert on a camel mare. These desert journey scenes involved an almost surreal evocation of the heat of the desert day; the terror of the night; the hunger, deprivation, and disorientation of the journey; and a confrontation with mortality—without consolation of an afterlife. The wearing away of the poet's self was often symbolized by the emaciation of the camel mare. Other desert animals—such as the oryx, onager, and ostrich—were depicted with a complex symbolic depth and poetic texture.

The final section, the boast, featured the reintegration of the poet into his tribe and the singing of the tribal values of generosity, courage in war, and the willingness to stand before death unflinchingly. The boast often was based on a poetic evocation of the sacrifice of the bedouin's camel and distribution of the meat to all the members of the tribe. The prime value was heroic generosity. The generous hero, the *Karīm*, was one who was willing to spend his fortune on a night's feast, to sacrifice his camel mare (symbolic of the self) for the tribe. Indeed, the camel sacrifice became the most important ritual and heroic moment in pre-Islamic Arabia. The *Karīm* also was willing to give his life in battle. Yet the celebration of the heroic ethos in the battle sections of the poems often revealed a tragic undertone. Even as the heroism was proclaimed, intimations arose of the tragedy of intertribal warfare and its open-ended cycle of killing and vengeance. Intuited within the deeper symbolism, verbal resonances, and intense imagery of the poem was the tragic effacement of the boundary of kin and non-kin, self and enemy. The killing of an enemy in battle (however heroically celebrated) led to an intimation of the fragility of kin boundaries (and boundaries between self and other) and the futility of a warfare that would end with the decimation of both tribes.

These odes are believed to have been composed, performed, and transmitted in an oral tradition similar to that of the jazz song or the Homeric epic, with each performance of a piece tailored, timed, and in part improvised to the audience. Gradually, the extraordinarily vivid images of the odes were configured in differing modes: comic, tragic, elegiac, ironic, and heroic. The development of these expressive modes led to the formation and discovery of a common nation. Different tribes speaking different dialects developed a common poetic language that expressed the range of human sentiment within shared cultural values and sensibilities. The notion of the Arab, as a name for the tribes speaking the Arabic language—not just in a lexical sense but in this more profound sense of common cultural bonds and expression—was being developed, even as the tragic element within the tribal heroic ethos was expressed and understood more deeply. The discovery of a common cultural bond among the tribes and an intimation of the tragic element in their cycles of warfare were culminating at the time the young man from Mecca heard what he understood to be revelations of God.[3]

The Qur'an retains key bedouin values such as remembrance, generosity, hospitality, and valor. But the social context for such values is transformed. The remembrance is no longer of a beloved and a lost tribal love affair, but of the deity who, even when figured in later poetry as a beloved, maintains a more explicitly transcendent character. The journey through the desert evolves into a moral and spiritual journey, a journey of the human being toward the divine lord. The generous hero, the *Karīm*, is still the model of human excellence, but the hero is no longer the tribal chief or even the prophet, but the all-giving deity and the human being who imitates that generosity by working for social justice.

The tradition of the tribal Qasida remained a powerful and resonant force within Arabian society for centuries. Indeed, along with the Qur'an, it provides the warp and woof of classical Arabic culture, sometimes serving as a counter text to the Qur'an, some-times as a mode of expression of Qur'anic values. Yet the role of the Qasida would never be quite the same after the the shift sym-bolized by the submission of Ka'b to Muhammad. Instead of being draped with the "Hanging Odes," the Ka'ba is now draped with another text embroidered on rare Egyptian cloth. That text con-tains quotes from the Qur'an, and the cloth that holds it, the Kiswa, has been a feature of the shrine in Mecca since the early Is-lamic period.

II. The Qur'an as Recitation

What was the spirit of those early Meccan verses that became cen-tral to the Qur'anic tradition? When the reader unfamiliar with Islam and unversed in Arabic picks up the standard English trans-lation of the Qur'an, that spirit can be hard to find. What the per-son who learns the Qur'an in Arabic experiences as a work of consummate power and beauty, outsiders can find difficult to grasp, confusing, and in most English translations, alienating. The written Qur'an does not seem to have a clear beginning, middle, and end. It shifts thematic registers: from mystical passages to sa-cred history, from law to the struggles of Muhammad and his fol-lowers with little or no warning. Many of its chapters mix themes that sometimes begin in mid-topic. The Suras are arranged in what can seem a chronologically and topically arbitrary manner, with the longest Suras at the beginning and the shortest at the end.

The experience of the Qur'an in traditional Islamic countries is very different from Western attempts to read it as a story bound within the pages of a book with a sequence of beginning, middle, and end. For Muslims, the Qur'an is first experienced in Arabic, even by those who are not native speakers of Arabic. In Qur'an schools, children memorize verses, then entire Suras. They begin with the Suras that are at the end of the Qur'an in its written form. These first revelations to Muhammad express vital existential themes in a language of great lyricism and beauty. As the students learn these Suras, they are not simply learning something by rote, but rather interiorizing the inner rhythms, sound patterns, and textual dynamics—taking it to heart in the deepest manner.

Gradually the student moves on to other sections of the Qur'an. Yet the pattern set by this early, oral encounter with the text is maintained throughout life. The Qur'anic experience is not the experience of reading a written text from beginning to end. Rather, the themes, stories, hymns, and laws of the Qur'an are woven through the life stages of the individual, the key moments of the community, and the sensual world of the town and village. Life is punctuated by the recitation of the Qur'an by trained reciters who speak from the minarets of mosques, on the radio, and from cassettes played by bus drivers, taxi drivers, and individuals. The experience is a nonlinear repetition through recitation. The actual stories, which may seem fragmented in a written version, are brought together in the mind of the hearer through repeated experiences with the text. The most accomplished Qur'anic reciters are famous throughout the Islamic world, and their cassettes and CDs can be found in kiosks and music stores in any city with a large Islamic population.

This Qur'anic experience is intertwined through Arabic literature and civilization and, in an extended fashion, through the arts and civilization of other non-Arab Islamic societies. Qur'anic calligraphy, the visual manifestation of the Qur'an, is the basis for Arabic calligraphy and one of the most distinctive features of Islamic architecture. Qur'anic inscriptions can be found on almost any major work of architecture, offering yet another form of remembrance (*dhikr*). Almost all of the major works of art in the Islamic world draw on Qur'anic allusions. To cite just one example, love poets consider the Qur'anic story of Moses, who was overwhelmed and nearly destroyed by his near vision of the deity, to be a model for the power and intensity of love. The subtlest allusion to Moses on Sinai is enough to conjure up the entire context.

Qur'anic sensibility grounds popular culture as well. As we will see later, Qur'anic phrases have become central to popular language. The relation of the Qur'an to popular culture also is exemplified by Umm Kulthum, an Arab singer who was one of the most important cultural figures in Islamic societies in the modern age. Her singing permeated the Arabic world. Her funeral was the

Muslim boys and girls are taught to read and memorize the early chapters of the Qur'an. Here a young boy is reading from the Qur'an.

largest public event in Egypt's modern history. Umm Kulthum's lyrics combined the tradition of Arabic love poetry, contemporary forms of music, and a cadence she learned as the the daughter of a rural Qur'an reciter. Umm Kulthum was also believed to have been an accomplished Qur'an reciter herself.[4] In buses, cafes, and taxis throughout the Arabic-speaking world, cassettes of the songs of Umm Kulthum are almost as popular as cassettes of the Qur'an.

III. The Early Meccan Suras

The Qur'an traditionally is divided into three periods: the early Meccan Suras (most of the short Suras at the end of the Qur'an and other Suras or parts of Suras scattered through the rest of the Qur'an), the later Meccan Suras, and the Medinan Suras. The Qur'anic texts commonly put the terms "Meccan" or "Medinan" after the title of each Sura to indicate the phase of Muhammad's life in which it was revealed. The early and later Meccan Suras are believed to have been revealed to Muhammad before he made his famous emigration (*hijra*) to Medina in the year 622 C.E., Year One of the Islamic or Hijrī calendar.[5]

The Suras from the early Meccan period focus on existential and personal issues. The later Meccan period brings in more extended discussions of sacred history and the prophets known in the Biblical traditions. The message of the Qur'an is more explicitly fitted into a prophetic lineage beginning with the creation of Adam, the first prophet in Islam, extending through the stories of Noah, Abraham, Isaac, Jacob, Joseph, Moses, John the Baptist, and Jesus, prophets of the Arab tradition such as Hud and Salih, and ending with Muhammad. The Suras from the Medinan period reflect Muhammad's new position as a political, economic, social, and military leader and so address a wider range of societal, historical, and legal issues. As ruler of a state, Muhammad was faced with an array of specific problems, some of which are answered with Qur'anic revelations.

As Muhammad's career advanced, the ritual core of Islam was more fully articulated within the Qur'an. Of the "five pillars" of Islamic practice, three were discussed in the early Meccan Suras: the affirmation of the oneness of God, the ritual prayer (salat), and the obligation to give a pure offering (zakāt) of one's wealth to those in need. In later periods, the number of prayers required per day was fixed at five and the orientation of the prayers was set toward the shrine of the Ka'ba in Mecca; the obligation for fasting during the month of Ramadan (the month the initial Qur'anic revelations are believed to have been sent down to Muhammad) was enjoined on all able adult Muslims; and, finally, the Islamic pilgrimage or hajj, which contained many of the elements of pre-Islamic pilgrimage activities around Mecca, was ordained for all Muslims capable of it.

For the first generations living after the death of Muhammad, issues of interpretation and communal life could be resolved by referring to the Qur'an or to what they knew Muhammad had said or done. This tradition of Muhammad's words and deeds is called the sunna (path, example) of the prophet. But as Islam extended further from its original community in Medina, it became more difficult to resolve such issues by informal appeal to the sunna. As a result, the statements of Muhammad outside of the Qur'an (hadīth) were rigorously examined and codified. The hadīth literature was then combined with the Qur'an and principles of legal judgment (*fiqh*) to elaborate an Islamic way of life, *sharī'a*, that would be valid in later times and more distant places. Such regulations could cover everything from dietary restrictions to details of family law, inheritance, divorce, and the ethics of investment and avoidance of predatory business practices. This world of codified principles of shari'a has been frequently compared to the rabbinic tradition that was codified in the Mishna and Talmud.

Although the Qur'an views itself as representing the prophetic tradition of Abraham, Moses, and Jesus, as a document the Qur'an is approached differently than the Torah or the Christian Bible. Most Jews and Christians acknowledge that the Biblical texts may have been composed by a wide variety of authors over a long period of time, under divine inspiration certainly, but not necessarily by direct speech of the deity. On the other hand, most Muslims view the Qur'an as the direct revelation of God to Muhammad. Muslim scholars, as well as many non-Muslim scholars, stipulate that the Qur'an was composed within the lifetime of one historical personage, Muhammad, and that many of the events of the Qur'an are reflections of the life and struggles of Muhammad.

Another key difference between Qur'anic and Biblical traditions is in narrative style. The Qur'an does not narrate the sacred history of the prophets in a linear fashion. With the exception of the account of the prophet Joseph (Sura 12), the Qur'an scatters its tales of the prophets throughout the text. Aspects of the story of Moses, for example, occur in 44 different passages in the Qur'an, but are never brought together in a single Sura. This Qur'anic way of storytelling, unusual to those accustomed to the Biblical tradition, has aroused a number of conflicting interpretations and value judgments. The polemicist Carlyle remarked, "With every allowance, one feels it difficult to see how any mortal ever could consider this Koran as a Book written in Heaven, too good for the Earth; as a well written-book, or indeed as a *book* at all." On the other hand, Norman O. Brown recently suggested that it is this very scattered or fragmented mode of composition that allows the Qur'an to achieve its most profound effects, as if the intensity of the prophetic message were shattering the vehicle of human language in which it was being communicated.[6]

To offer an account or overview of the entire Qur'an would require several volumes. The purpose here is to introduce the early
revelations, those that ground the rest of the Qur'an and are most
deeply embedded in Islamic life. When Muslims encounter the
early Suras of the Qur'an, they encounter the early life and career
of Muhammad. They learn about Muhammad's life as it is
reflected in Qur'anic discourses on the ephemeral nature of
human life, on the inevitability of a judgment on each human's
life, and on fundamental values. In this spirit, rather than offering
a detailed historical narrative, this volume presents the early Meccan Suras and offers explanatory comments that relate the Suras to
the life and culture of the prophet.

The early Meccan Suras are hymnic. The complex Qur'anic
sound patterns and the relation of sound to meaning—what we
might call the "sound vision" of the Qur'an—are brought out and
cultivated in Qur'anic recitation. No translation can fully capture
this sound vision. The translation here attempts to bring across the
lyricism of the hymnic passages, a lyricism comparable to that of
the Psalms or passages from the Upanishads. In the Qur'anic context, the lyricism is related to the use of oaths involving a key set
of what the Qur'an considers "signs" (āyas), clues to the mystery of
reality. These signs include the patterns of day and night, male and
female, odd and even, singular and plural. The Arabic construction
for these oaths can be translated in a number of ways. I have used
the phrase "by the," as in Sura 89: 1-5:

By the dawn
By the nights ten
By the odd and the even
By the night as it eases away
Is there not in that an oath for the thoughtful mind [7]

The values presented in the very early Meccan revelations are
repeated throughout the hymnic Suras. There is a sense of directness and intimacy, as if the hearer were being asked repeatedly a
simple question: what will be of value at the end of a human life?

The framework for this question is the concept of a final moment of truth or day of reckoning (*yawm ad-dīn*) in which each human being will face what he or she has done and has not done. The premise of these passages is that the human being avoids the ultimate question through self-delusion and avoids acknowledging his own mortality by engaging in the pursuit of wealth and possessions—"thinking in his wealth he will never die," as one Qur'anic verse puts it. The criticism of hoarding, the hoarding of one's possessions or one's life, was a standard in pre-Islamic Arabic poetry. The Qur'an keeps the value of the generous hero (the *Karīm*) but redefines generosity. The key value of generosity is no longer to be shown through camel sacrifice, great feasts, or giving one's life in tribal warfare. Rather, it is to be channeled into a concern for social justice, a continual willingness to give a share of one's possessions to the less fortunate. This giving is a purification of oneself and one's possessions as well as a recognition that no one truly owns anything. The Qur'anic *zakāt* (literally, "purification") is a purification of wealth in a ritual, communal, religious, and institutional sense through the organized giving and working for social justice. In the early Meccan Suras, the mechanisms and details of the obligation for *zakāt* are not yet worked out, but the importance of the obligation is made existentially present. The larger injunction to work for justice and the criticism of those who do not seek justice are categorical, as when the divine voice speaks of humankind in the following terms (Sura 90: 5-16):

> Does he think there is no power over him
> He says: look at the goods I devoured
> Does he think no one sees him

> Did we not endow him with eyes
> lips and tongue
> and guide him to the two high plains

> And he did not climb the steep pass
> What can tell you of the steep pass?

> To free a slave
> To feed the destitute on a day of hunger

a kinsman orphaned
or a stranger out of luck in need

A second premise of this ultimate question is that humans tend to hide, from others and from themselves, what they really are, but that Allah, the one God, sees into the inner being of each person and at the moment of truth will reveal each person, inside and out (Sura 100:11).

This day of judgment or moment of truth is an ontological reversal. What seems secure and lasting—the skies, the seas, the stars, the reality of death as contained in graves—is torn away. What seemed inconsequential—a "mote's weight" of good or a "mote's weight" of wrong (Sura 99:7-8)—is revealed as enduring and real. A classic example of such a moment is announced in Sura 82:1-5:

When the sky is torn
When the stars are scattered
When the seas are poured forth
When the tombs are burst open
Then a soul will know what it has given
    and what it has held back

The Qur'an does not propound a doctrine of the original or essential sinfulness of humanity. Human beings are not born sinful, but they are forgetful. This forgetfulness can be countered only by reminder (dhikr), which the Qur'an calls itself. Qur'anic dhikr includes repeated questioning about the primary Qur'anic values: sharing one's wealth; attending to the orphan, the destitute, and the disinherited; performing the prayer; and carrying out just deeds (salihāt).

The proper and continual performance of ritual prayer (salāt) is urged throughout the early Meccan Suras. Although the early Suras do not offer detailed prescriptions for the prayer, salāt is a performance of sujūd, the movement of worship in which the person first kneels and then touches the head to the ground. This movement, performed regularly, breaks the cycle of normal preoccupations, enacts humility, and helps in the remembrance of more ultimate concerns.

Finally, the affirmation of the oneness of God is given voice in Sura 112. The oneness of God has a number of interpretations in Islamic thought. First, of course, it means that the deity has no partners or equals. Second, in the moral sense, it has been interpreted as having no other aims, goals, or thoughts beyond the one reality or one deity. In other words, any other object that becomes an end in itself is a form of false deity. Third, in the theological sense, it can refer to the interior unity of the deity, that in God all the attributes—such as seeing, hearing, knowing, and willing—are in some sense one; that in God, willing is knowing and knowing is creating, although these activities seem separate within language. For some Islamic theologians, to give the deity separate attributes threatens the unity of God. If those attributes are eternal, then there is a diversity of eternal, separate powers. If they are not eternal, then God can change— a notion many Islamic philosophers, influenced by Aristotelian ideas on the impassivity of deity, found inconceivable. Fourth and finally, in many mystical theologies, unity involves knowing and seeing nothing but the one deity, or arriving at a point where a person's own existence actually passes away into the infinite reaches of that one God that is all that truly is.

The Qur'anic reminders of a basic ethic are placed within a framework of lyrical meditation and existential confrontation. At the heart of the early Suras is a voice that expresses at once a sense of intimacy and awe. It is this combination of intimacy and awe that I have tried to make accessible to those who do not encounter the Qur'an in the original Arabic recitation.

Within the nuances of Qur'anic language one encounters a balanced and powerful gender dynamic. Arabic, like French, is based on grammatical gender; even inanimate objects are masculine or feminine. The Qur'an uses this grammatical gender in a way that allows the masculine and feminine to move beyond the grammatical gender and form a kind of subtle gender interplay. Using condensed masculine or feminine grammatical constructions, fitting them into key places of rhyme and rhythm, and aligning them with certain implicit metaphors (the earth—grammatically feminine—giving birth to her final secret), the Qur'an generates a sense of gender interplay that always hovers at the edge of personification. The earth, the sky, the night of destiny, the soul, the sun, and the moon, for example, are all grammatically feminine. These terms are not openly personified, but are pushed toward personification through an implied metaphor (the night of destiny becomes pregnant, the earth gives birth at the day of reckoning) and rhetorical structures.

In order to bring across the supple gender language of the Qur'an, a translator must render the pronouns signifying inanimate objects carefully. If they are translated consistently in a gendered way (as her and him, she and he), the grammatical gender would be distorted into a blatant personification not there in the original text. But if they are translated in a neutered fashion, as is done in many standard translations of the Qur'an, some of the most moving and profound aspects of the Qur'anic voice themselves are neutered. In the commentaries, I have indicated areas where I have chosen one direction or another—that is, where I have tried to walk a balance among the gender registers.

Finally, the Qur'anic voice shifts continually. Sometimes the One God is referred to in the plural first person as "we"; sometimes in the third person as "your lord," "Allah," or "him/it"; and sometimes in the first person singular as "I." These sudden shifts can be disorienting at first, but they have an important literary and theological dimension. The shifts prevent the deity from becoming defined in anthropomorphic terms. Given the way finite human characteristics are built into the structure of language, a single, constant form of reference would lead to a reified deity—an intellectual idol in the terms of Islamic theologians and mystics. In the Qur'an the divine voice is heard in a variety of manners through an extraordinary range of emotions and tones, but the form or image of the speaker is never defined—a literary feature that mirrors the Qur'anic affirmation that the one God is beyond being fixed in any delimited form or image.

Each Qur'anic Sura is preceded by the phrase, "In the name of God the Compassionate the Caring" or alternatively "In the name of God the Compassionate Caring" (*bi smi Allāh ar-Raḥmān ar-Raḥīm*). This phrase is frequently translated, "In the name of God the Compassionate the Merciful," but traditional scholars have emphasized that the terms *Raḥmān* and *Raḥīm* are based upon an Arabic etymology linked to the word for womb (*raḥm*). In addition, "mercy" as a quality of forgiveness has been strongly marked by Christian associations with the doctrine of original sin, whereas the Qur'an does not posit the notion of original sin. For these reasons, and for the purposes of euphony and alliteration, I have used the translation "the Compassionate the Caring."[8]

As noted earlier, I have attached a facing commentary to each Sura which takes up issues of interpretation, historical context, and key themes. When young Muslims learn the Qur'an, they learn the text orally, often before they know Arabic grammar or the history of Islam. There is a tolerance for terms or concepts that are not fully understood but can be appreciated within the context of the hymnic nature of the text. For this reason, it is worthwhile to read the text before reading the commentaries.

I have used the term "translation" here to refer to the English renditions presented in this volume. But the term itself is controversial. For Muslims the Qur'an is, as expressed in Sura 12:2, an Arabic revelation. To understand the practical implications of such an understanding, one can turn to Africa. There, Christian missionaries begin by translating the Bible into the native language of the area. In many cases these translators have been forced to invent an orthography for an essentially oral language and tradition. By contrast, Muslim missionaries begin by opening a Qur'an school in which the Qur'an is taught in Arabic. The goal is not to replace the local language, but to introduce the Qur'an in Arabic in the way that (in the view of the majority of Muslims) it truly exists. The primary encounter of most Muslims with the Qur'an throughout their lives is in Arabic; for many that encounter centers on the Suras presented here.

In a later chapter of this book, I have offered a full transliteration of six short Suras, accompanied by a word-for-word English gloss. Those who do not know Arabic can follow the Arabic recitation on the enclosed CD with the help of the transliteration and gloss. I have made a practice of introducing in my classes a few Suras, with transliterations, English glosses, and recitations played on CD or cassette. Although only a small part of the Qur'an can be covered this way in a classroom setting, this method allows an encounter with the sound vision central to the Qur'an.

The translations and commentaries presented here are the result of fifteen years of work on these particular Suras and my experience attempting to present them in classes of non-Arabic speakers. Each Sura has gone through dozens of drafts. A translator is constantly forced to choose between terms that can only partially carry the full connotations of the original, between keeping or losing key literary affects (such as rhyme, interior assonance, and rhythmic movements), and somehow making compensation for elements that have to be given up in certain choices.

Of course, all translations are ultimately only approaches. One can never completely recapture an original in a new language. For some, adhering to a facile interpretation of the Italian cliché *traduttore traditore* (translator-traitor), the impossibility of perfect translation only shows the futility of trying. My own view is that translation—never complete, always only an approach—is an essential element of human existence. Even among those who speak our own language, we often find we have interpreted a word in a way other than it was intended. We can fully never capture or seize the perfected meaning. If we could grasp or seize it, we would soon find that the meaning has lost its magic in captivity. But the always renewed effort to come as close as possible is a reward in itself. For both theological and literary reasons, the Qur'an is particularly resistant to any notion of translation as a complete reproduction of the meaning and form of the original; what follows does not presume to be such a translation.

The history of English renditions of the Qur'an has been marked by the transference of the language of the King James Bible onto the Qur'anic text. Yet that idiom grew out of a literary tradition that was itself rooted in the Bible. To impose it on a completely different kind of text risks producing a language that is artificial or awkward, despite its scholarly accomplishment. The version presented here does away with some of the grander features of King

James rhetoric, particularly in the use of interjections, references to deity, and theologically motivated capitalization. It attempts an English that is natural and relatively idiomatic, yet formal enough to reflect certain high registers of Qur'anic diction.

But beyond these issues of translation style, another issue more deeply interweaves language and theology. A standard stereotype about Islam and the Qur'an, one that has been propounded by anti-Muslim polemicists and missionaries, is that Islam is a religion of fear as opposed to Christianity, for example, which is (in their view) a religion of love. For Muslims familiar with the Qur'an in Arabic, the notion that it is centered on fear is not only inaccurate but astounding. Certainly, the Qur'anic emphasis on justice is continually intertwined in the early Meccan Suras with the affirmation of an ultimate meaning in life. At the day of reckoning, this meaning and justice are brought together. The Qur'an warns those who reject the day of reckoning and who are entrenched in lives of acquisition and injustice that an accounting awaits them.[10] Yet these warnings are not more dire or grim than the warnings the Biblical Jesus gives in the parables about burning and gnashing of teeth. And in Qur'anic recitation, all Qur'anic passages on alienation between humankind and God are dominated by a tone, not of anger or wrath, but of sadness (*ḥuzn*). Why, then, have the deeper resonances and reaches of these passages been reduced to only one aspect—that of warning?

One reason for this distorted emphasis is the way the early Meccan Suras were interpreted in the Middle Ages. Just as medieval Christians constructed an elaborate vision of the torments of hell from enigmatic statements in the Bible, so medieval Qur'anic commentators constructed their own visions of hell and heaven from the elliptic comments in the Quran about the day of reckoning. Yet, when one reads the early Meccan Suras, one finds that these references are of a literary and psychological subtlety and suppleness at odds with the spatially and temporally fixed notions of heaven and hell, reward and punishment.

The issue was epitomized by the Islamic writer Qushayri, who made crucial distinctions between fear and hope on the one hand, and awe on the other.[11] Fear and hope are emotions that concern the future. Awe is an emotion or feeling that concerns the present. In a state of awe, a person is no longer even thinking about the future. What gives the early Meccan Suras their depth, psychological subtlety, texture, and tone is the way the future is collapsed into the present; the way the day of reckoning is transferred from the fear and hope of a moment in the future to a sense of reckoning in the present moment. The centrality of the day of reckoning to the early Qur'anic revelations is based on a prophetic impulse to remind humanity of the moment of truth. The impulse of reminder (*dhikr*) is not simply to talk about that moment, but allow the hearer to live and experience in this present moment the existential absoluteness of a mote's weight of good or evil.

In creating such a sense of the moment, the early Meccan Suras employ a distinctive way of referring to the day of reckoning and the afterlife or finality (*al-akhira*). There are references to the garden, *'Iliyyīn*, the fire, *Jaḥīm*, and *Jehenna* (a term related to the Biblical term *Gehenna* used for a pit of the dead and later as a term for punishment in the afterlife). But these references are placed in an allusive and elusive literary frame that gives them a depth far beyond any simple-minded notion of heavenly reward and hellish punishment. Indeed, the references to the day of reckoning are filled with key syntactical ambiguities that translators and commentators often remove, thus simplifying and freezing the text. When those ambiguities are respected, the day of reckoning passages become centered on a kind of questioning—a questioning that combines a sense of awe with a sense of intimacy. This translation and the accompanying commentaries focus on keeping the original sense of questioning alive in English.

One example of such questioning occurs in the Sura of the Qāri'a. The Sura includes two mysterious words, *qāri'a* (a word that could mean smashing, obliterating, crushing, or calamity), and *hāwiya* (a word that means variously a mother who has lost her first-born child, desire, abyss, and falling). The Sura begins with three staccato references to the *qāri'a*. It then asks what can tell what the *qāri'a* is. However it does not define the *qāri'a*. Instead it speaks of the day in which the *qāri'a* occurs as a day in which mountains are like fluffed tufts of wool and human beings like scattered moths—an image evocative of the inversion of strong and weak that is characteristic of the early revelations.

The ending section of the Sura begins with a reference to the person whose mother is *hāwiya*. This reference has a range of connotations, including the loss experienced by the mother, the existential negation of the child whose mother has lost her child, and the more general sense of falling and abyss. Then the Qur'an asks what can tell us of the *hāwiya*. The next verse says simply "raging fire." There is a crucial ambiguity in syntax here between the two verses. Is raging fire something that can give us a glimpse of what the *hāwiya* is? Or is the raging fire to be equated with the *hāwiya*? As explained below, the power of these images is heightened by the "sound figure" created around the Arabic expression *hā*. The sound *hā* can mean "her," but it is a sound that occurs in interjections of sorrow and surprise. This sound is also the central sound figure in the Sura, culminating in its being part of the mysterious term *hāwiya*, a term that in some sense breaks apart under the stress of sound and meaning at this key moment in the text.

The Calamity (The *Qári'a*)
> In the Name of God the Compassionate the Caring
>> The *qári'a*
>> What is the *qári'a*
>> What can tell you of the *qári'a*
>> A day humankind are like moths scattered
>> And mountains are like fluffs of wool
>> Whoever's scales weigh heavy
>> His is a life that is pleasing
>> Whoever's scales weigh light
>> His mother is *háwiya*
>> What can let you know what she is
>> Raging fire.

Most commentators and translators have explained away or covered over the ambiguity and simply equated the *hāwiya* with fire. They have also changed the text to "*the* fire," interpolating into it a definite article that does not exist in the Qur'anic text itself. They explain further that the word *hāwiya* is simply a name for "the fire"; in other words, another name for hell. In the reduction of the word *hāwiya* to a synonym for hell, psychological complexity is lost. The reflection on the meaning of *hāwiya*, the resonances of a woman bereft of her child, an abyss, an infinite depth of desire, a falling into that depth, and, finally, the evocative ambivalence of those meanings in relationship to raging fire, are all reduced to a monotonic threat of punishment. Little wonder that many readers seeing the text in English have focused upon the notion of threat for those who misbehave, a notion that is hardly original or distinctive, and have missed the deeper questioning, literary power, and psychological subtlety of such passages.

The intimacy and awe evoked by early Meccan accounts of the day of reckoning are typical of all the Qur'anic passages that bring up the issue of spirit (*rūḥ*). In the Qur'an, spirit is associated with three moments: the creation of Adam through God's breathing; the coming down of prophecy, as on the night of destiny and especially in the prophethood of Jesus and Muhammad; and, finally, the day of reckoning. These three moments are boundary moments, that is, moments in which time meets that which is beyond time. Insofar as they converge in a world beyond time, the three moments of spirit collapse into one another.

My approach to the Qur'an presumes to make no judgment on the ultimate truth of these texts, which are among the more influential in human history. It engages them with the respect for literary and theological depth that a translator gains through repeated efforts to recreate some sense of the original. In that spirit, this volume is meant for a varied audience: for those who have wished to know something about Islam and who have little background in its history; for those who wish to study or teach the Qur'an in a classroom setting; and for Muslims who may find this version to capture some aspects of the text in a relevant way or who wish to share an approach to the Qur'an that is accessible with non-Muslim friends. My goal is to present in English some of the texture, tone, power, and subtlety of the Arabic text that is the Qur'an.

In any translation, there is a loss and an effort to compensate for that loss. Some features in the original cannot be duplicated in the new language without artificiality. Thus, for example, there is no possibility of duplicating the end-rhymes in many Qur'anic passages in an English idiom in which rhyming is far more difficult and would require forced and awkward syntax. I have attempted to find compensations through assonance, partial rhyme, and other features more natural to current English idiom. You will note in the translations a minimum of punctuation. Classical Arabic does not use punctuation. In addition, these early Qur'anic Suras are at their most compelling when the exact relationship of one statement to another hangs in a balance and, instead of freezing into some clearly definable meaning, continues to resonate and pose questions that only a lifetime of searching can answer. The Suras are rendered in such a way that each line beginning flush left is a new verse. Any indentation indicates that the indented line is part of the previous verse. In this way, the verses can be indicated less obtrusively (with numbers of 5, 10, 15, etc. in the margin) and the reader can easily calculate the verse number of any line.

There are aspects of the Qur'an that elude translation and compensations, particularly those aspects focused on what I have called sound figures. In the facing commentaries and in the final chapters I discuss these aspects of Qur'anic language. In other works written in a more technical style, I have placed my understanding of Qur'anic sound figures within the traditional world of Qur'anic scholarship.[12] While the translations and commentary I offer are grounded in traditional scholarship, they also represent my personal understanding of the literary character of the Qur'an in areas (such as sound figures) that were not highlighted by Qur'anic commentators.

The early Meccan passages draw the hearer into a world of elemental transformations. Rather than limiting themselves to describing a future event (promise and threat), these passages make present the event in question. At the key point in the text, the language opens up around a semantic abyss. The event takes on immediacy. It is this immediacy that accounts for such diverse reactions as the German scholar Nöldeke's, who describes the effect of the Sura of the Calamity as making one feel "as if he saw with his own eyes," and Fakhr ad-Dīn Rāzī's, who speaks of the word *qāriʿa* in that Sura as overpowering "our hearts with the sense of awe."[13]

The proclamatory aspects of the early Meccan passages, the strange vocabulary, the semantic gaps, and the cosmic perspective establish a distance between text and audience. However, within the elusive discourse of sound figures that distance is both enhanced and overcome. As the proclamatory surface of the text "breaks apart" into sound figures, clustered basic sound units and implied personifications, a new tone is heard: whisperings, inferences, highly personal intonations of emotion and gender. It is as if the speaker, the hearer, and the subject of discourse were intimately known to one another; awe and intimacy are brought together.

Qur'anic reciters and commentators characterize the tone of the Qur'anic recitation as one of sadness (*ḥuzn*). This is not a world-rejecting sadness. Indeed, the sadness is at its most telling in those passages in which the world's mystery and splendor are evoked. Yet there is a sense that somehow the splendor and mystery are too great for the human to encompass—or that the human heart has somehow forgotten it actually has the capacity to encompass that splendor and mystery. At this moment of reminder, the text expresses not fear but the sadness that comes with a personal realization of a loss that is part of the human condition. The day of reckoning contains the possibility that this loss will be overcome with a final reconciliation and sense of belonging, or that it will be revealed as permanent—and it brings into the present the reality of that moment of finality.[14] This combination of a sense of awe with interior whisperings of intimacy and sadness may help account for the broadness of appeal of the early Meccan Suras as well as their distinctiveness as a form of apocalyptic language.[15]

Footnotes

1. Such an approach is rejected by those who accept the Qur'anic assertions that it was revealed directly to Muhammad, just as the effort to show multiple authors and historical periods for the first five books of the Bible is rejected by those in Biblical tradition who adhere most strongly to the view that the entire Torah was revealed by God to Moses. For a popular overview of developments and controversies in this particular area of Qur'anic studies, see Toby Lester, "What is the Qur'an," *The Atlantic Monthly* 23.1 (January, 1999), pp. 43-56.

2. See Richard Bulliet, *The Camel and the Wheel* (Cambridge, MA: Harvard University Press, 1976). The fact that Arabia, because of its oil deposits, has once again become vital to the world's transportation system is an irony most dramatically illustrated by the bedouin who use four-wheel drive pick-up trucks to carry newly birthed camels and food for their camel herds.

3. See Michael Sells, *Desert Tracings: Six Classic Arabian Odes* (Middletown, CT: Wesleyan University Press, 1989); Jaroslav Stetkevych, *Muhammad and the Golden Bough* (Bloomington: Indiana University Press, 1996); and Suzanne Stetkevych, *The Mute Immortals Speak* (Ithaca, NY: Cornell University Press, 1993); see also Suzanne Stetkevych, *Reorientations: Arabic and Persian Poetry* (Bloomington: Indiana University Press, 1994).

4. For recent work on Umm Kulthum, see Virginia Danielson, *The Voice of Egypt: Umm Kulthum, Arabic Song, and Egyptian Society in the Twentieth Century* (Chicago: University of Chicago Press, 1997); and the film *Umm Kulthum: A Voice Like Egypt* (Waltham, MA : Filmmakers Collaborative, 1996).

5. Because the Islamic calendar is based on the lunar calendar, each Islamic year is shorter than the solar year and calculating the correspondence of Islamic calendars to the Common Era (c.e.) calendar requires a complex formula. When authors use both systems, they usually put the Islamic year first. Thus the famous mystic Ibn 'Arabi is said to have died in the year 638/1240. The letter H (for Hijri) is sometimes used to indicate the Islamic year: 638H/1240 c.e.

6. The quote from Carlyle is cited in Norman O. Brown, "The Apocalypse of Islam," *Social Text* 3:8 (1983-84): 155-171, the same article in which Brown gives his defense of the nonlinear character of Qur'anic discourse.

7. Alternative translations could be as simple as "and" as in "and the dawn," or as complex as "I swear by the dawn" or "I summon the dawn,"

or even, in agreement with usage in Arabic poetry, "how many a dawn."

8. These issues are described in more detail, with extended quotations from Islamic thinkers, in Michael Sells, *Early Islamic Mysticism* (New York: Paulist Press, Classics of Western Spirituality), 1996, pp. 304-320.

9. The word *Allāh* is a proper noun in Arabic, thought to be based upon the phrase "the god" (*al-ilāh*). It is as if the definite article "the" had been partially squeezed into the word for deity. Considered as a proper name, it cannot, of course, be translated. But to render it Allah, in the context of a translation of the Qur'an, sets up a factor of alienation. For Muslims, the Allah of the Qur'an is the same God as the God of Abraham, Moses, and Jesus. Although in other contexts, it may be wise to keep the term Allah, or to vary between Allah and God, in this context it is vital not to set up a factor of alienation at the beginning.

10. In addition to its arrangement by Suras, the Qur'an also is arranged by parts. Each part (*juz'*) is the amount that should be recited in a day's recitation. This arrangement is by volume of text. The last part of the Qur'an, called the *juz' 'amma* after its first two words, consists of Suras 78-114. I have presented here—in addition to The Opening and the key vision verses of Sura 53—Suras 84-114 in full and in sequence. Of them, Suras 98 and 110 (and 99, though this is more controversial) are considered to be of a later period, but I have left them in to show the contrast with the later period and to give the full sequence of this section of the Qur'an.

I present here what I think would make a good introduction to the Qur'an, without attempting to introduce the entire *juz' 'amma*, the first Suras of which bring up issues that go beyond the boundaries of this volume. For an important interpretation and rendition of the entire *juz' 'amma*, see *The Awesome News, Interpetation of Juz' 'Amma —The Last Part of the Qur'an*, second edition, by Dr. Mahmoud M. Ayoub (n.p.: World Islamic Call Society, second edition, 1997).

11. The importance and usefulness of fear of punishment and desire for reward is a controversial issue in Islamic history. Some major theologians, such as Hasan al-Basri and al-Ghazali, believed that contemplation of the terrors of punishment and the bliss of rewards were essential to refining the human conscience. On the other hand, the famous mystic Rabi'a denounced any activity done out of fear of divine punishment or desire for divine rewards. She is known for a story in which she was seen walking down the street with a vessel of water in one hand and a fire in the other. When asked what she was going to do with the water and fire, she stated that she would burn paradise with the fire and douse the flames of hell with the water, so that never again would

anyone act out of anything other than pure love of God. Both perspectives, of course, are steeped in the Qur'an.

12. See Sells, *Early Islamic Mysticism*, pp. 103-110.

13. M. Sells, "Sound, Spirit, and Gender in *Sūrat al-Qadr*," *Journal of the American Oriental Society*, 11.2 (September, 1990): 101-139; *idem*, "Sound and Meaning in Sūrat al-Qāri'a," *Arabica*, 40 (1993): 403-430; and *idem*, "A Literary Approach to the Hymnic Suras of the Qur'an," in Issa Boullata, ed., *Literary Structures of Religious Meaning in the Qur'an* (London: Curzon Press), in press. This volume is devoted to understanding and appreciating the literary aspects of the Qur'an. *Approaching the Qur'an* makes no attempt to adduce a catechism or doctrine of the Qur'an, nor does it claim any legal or religious authority or sponsorship.

14. Fakhr ad-Dīn ar-Razi, *at-Tafsīr al-Kabīr* (*The Great Commentary*), vol. 32 (Cairo: Itizām 'Abd ar-Rahman Muhammad, n.d.), p. 71.

15. *Huzn* is acknowledged by Qur'anic reciters as a major element in the recitation, and classical writers refer to it anecdotally. At times it is reduced to a subservient category to threat. I view the quality of sadness not as an aspect of threat but as an emotion evoked at the moment that threat opens up onto more complex emotive possibilities through the transformation of semantic and temporal categories —when the sense of loss is experienced in the present rather than as a threat of future punishment.

16. The early Meccan Suras, such as the Sura of the *Qāri'a* may well share apocalyptic elements, common themes, images, and even vocabulary with other literatures or traditions. But the literary effect is due to the specific employment within the Sura of a complex set of interpermeating discursive modes. In calling this style distinctive, I am not suggesting it is unique. Such a claim would demand detailed comparative analysis with all the relevant apocalyptic material that has survived and all that may have been lost.

The first chapter of the Qur'án,
Súrat al-Fātiḥa, The Opening.

Glossary

Annotated Glossary
of Key Concepts

Day of Reckoning (*yawm ad-dīn*). This is the primary subject of the early Meccan Suras. The word translated here as reckoning (*dīn*) is related to a number of terms for borrowing and payment of debt, as well as to terms for religion and faith. The word for day (*yawm*) also can be a more general term for any length of time or a moment in time. The term has been translated as "day of judgment" and "day of accounting." But it also has an implication similar to the "moment of truth"—that is, a time of indeterminate duration in which each soul will encounter the fundamental reality that normal consciousness masks. At that moment each person will know what he or she has given and held back, and every "mote's weight" of kindness or meanness will take on its status as one's true self and destiny in a moment of revelation and finality.

Deniers, Those in Denial, Those Who Call It (the day of reckoning) a Lie (*al-mukadhdhibūn*). Those who repeatedly reject prophetic messages, in particular the message of the day of reckoning, are those who put themselves outside the possibility of just relations among humans or between the human and the divine. The word for unbelievers (*kāfirūn*) has connotations both of concealing and of ingratitude. The unbelievers are depicted as active deniers (*mukadhdhibūn*) who are not content with refusing to assent to certain Qur'anic understandings, but who actively persecute those who do.

Generous Hero (*karīm*). Heroic generosity was the centerpiece of pre-Islamic Arabian tribal values. The generous hero (*karīm*) was one who would spend his fortune and sacrifice his camel mare (the most important possession and a symbol of himself) to feed others. He would give his life in battle. He would, in hyperbolic display, spend a fortune on a night of revelry with his friends. By contrast, hoarding (of one's wealth or one's life) was the fundamental mark of ignobility.

In the Qur'an, the central place of generosity is affirmed. On the day of reckoning, people will be asked what they have given and what they have held back, but the context of the generosity has shifted. Tribal warfare was outlawed. The pre-Islamic camel sacrifice yielded to the great sacrifice in honor of Abraham (introduced in later sections of the Qur'an). And the hyperbolic display of generosity was transformed into a socially mandated offering for those in society who are in need: in particular, the orphan, the widow, those lacking strong kin connections, and the traveler. The Qur'an turns the pre-Islamic satire against the greedy and ungenerous into a more existential critique, asking mordantly if those who consume their lives acquiring things think that their possessions will make them immortal (Sura 104).

Yet this human generosity is seen only as a proper response of human beings in sharing what has been given to them by the only true *karīm* in Qur'anic thought: Allah or God. "Karīm" is one of the principle "names of God" in the Qur'an and, because Muslims frequently take as their given name one of the names of God,

Karīm and 'Abd al-Karīm (Servant of the Generous) have become popular names in Islamic societies.

Faith (*imān*). The word translated as "faith," *imān*, means more than assent to certain beliefs. It entails an active witness, as manifested in performing just works, carrying out the ritual prayer, and giving the pure offering (*zakāt*)—often in the face of adversity, mockery, persecution, and other difficulties. For this reason, I have used the English term "keep the faith" rather than the more abstract and passive "believe" for the many verbal expressions referring to "those who keep the faith" (*āmanū*). The word also carries connotations of safety, trust, and peace.

Humankind, Human Being Person, Someone (*insān*). The word *insān* refers to humankind in general, but also, in many instances, to any person, someone, or anyone. In the the translations below, when words like "anyone" or "someone" are used, they carry also the connotation of humankind, and when words for humankind are used, they can also be the more specific reference to any person as a representative of humankind. *Insān* is gender non-specific, but has traditionally been translated into English as "man" or "mankind," in accordance with traditional English language use of the word "man" in an intended gender non-specific sense. However, because the etymology and flavor of a word has a power beyond the intention of a human author or translator, to declare the English word "man" gender non-specific is not enough to overcome the set of associations (manhood, manly, be a man) that its use will invoke, at least subliminally. In order to preserve the intricate gender balance within the Qur'an, I have translated *insān* in gender non-specific terms throughout.

Jinn, Genies (sing. *jinnī*, pl. *jinn*). The Qur'an addresses itself to two species of sentient and rational beings: humankind and jinn. The *jinn*—semi-spirit beings translated in English as "genies"—are affirmed by the Qur'an as a fundamental aspect of the created world. In pre-Islamic Arabia, the *jinn* were associated with love, madness, and poetic inspiration. They could appear to the desert traveler in a variety of forms, lure him off the path, and destroy him. The power of the *jinn* is immense, but they are neither pure light like the angels nor pure evil; indeed, the Qur'an presents the jinn, like humans, as embracing or refusing Islam. One species of *jinn* was known as the satans (*shaytāns*). This figure is believed to have been transformed into a more purely malevolent being in Arabic folk culture and is associated in the Qur'an with the fallen heavenly being known as Iblīs.

Just Deeds (*ṣāliḥāt*). These constitute one of the major ethical injunctions of the early Meccan Suras, the other being keeping the faith. Several clear examples are given of carrying out just acts: feeding the poor, sheltering the homeless, protecting the orphan, defending the infant female child from infanticide, and urging others to join together to carry out such acts. The Qur'anic emphasis on just acts is repeatedly tied to ultimate questions of the meaning and justice of life itself as exemplified in the final reckoning or moment of truth.

Mindfulness (*taqwā*). The Qur'anic term *taqwā* derives from an Arabic root meaning "to shield oneself." It refers to consciousness of the divine, along with alert concern to avoid the egoism, injustice, and forgetfulness to which humankind is prone. The term has sometimes been translated as "fear of the lord," but the stress in the early Meccan Suras is less on fear than on vigilance. Later moral philosophers in Islam, such as Muhasibi, analyzed the subtlety and insidiousness of egoism in profound psychological detail as a way of explaining and exploring the Qur'anic emphasis on mindfulness.

Patience (*ṣabr*). The voice of the Qur'an continually evokes the need for patience. The prophet needs patience in the face of rejection of his message. Human beings need patience in the face of persecution or obstruction in their effort to "keep the faith and work justice." The deity exercises patience in allowing those who are unjust to prosper for a time. The Qur'an assures those who are suffering hardship that "after every hard time there is an easing."

Prayer (*ṣalāt*). The ritual prayer or *ṣalāt* enjoined in the early Meccan Suras is based on *sujūd*, in which a person first bows, then kneels, then touches the head to the ground in worship. A series of such movements is called a *rak'a*. Later Qur'anic passages defined more specifically the ritual prayer, set the number of observances at five times per day, and fixed the orientation of the prayer toward the Ka'ba. The prayer is a form of remembrance that encompasses spirit, mind, and body. It is meant to break into normal human preoccupations and reorient a person to matters of ultimate concern. Islam includes other forms of prayer (petitions, intimate conversations with the deity), but when the term prayer is used in the Qur'an, it almost always refers to the ritual prayer of *ṣalāt*.

Muslims have explained the sense of peace and tranquility gained by performing the prayer in a variety of ways: comparing the movements to Yogic positions, the physical position to that of an infant in the womb, and touching the ground to an act of humility and an acknowledgment that the human is part of the world of creation.

Pure Offering (*zakāt*). In addition to keeping the faith, carrying out just deeds, and performing the ritual prayer, the early Meccan Suras command the *zakāt*. The etymology of *zakāt* is associated primarily with purity, and secondarily with flourishing or growth. In giving a share of one's property, in an organized fashion (rather than in a tribal feast) to those in need, a person purifies both self and property. The concept of *zakāt* was defined further in later Qur'anic revelations and became one of the five pillars of Islamic life, institutionalized as a form of tithing obligatory on all Muslims. Note that when the words for prayer and offering, *ṣalā* and *zakā*, stand independently, they are pronounced without a final "t", but when it is used with a following word, the "t" is frequently added. However, because it has become standard in English works to keep the "t", I have followed that precedent and hereafter use the "t" in referring to both terms.

Remembrance (*dhikr*). This is one of the core concepts of the Qur'an and of Islamic civilization. Remembrance of the beloved formed the first section of the classical Arabic ode, the major form of expression in pre-Islamic Arabia. In the Qur'an, *dhikr* is both reminder and remembrance. The Qur'an refers to itself as a reminder to humankind. Islamic rituals, such as the obligatory prayer, are forms of reminder. The recitation of the Qur'an and Qur'anic calligraphy are sensibly embodied forms of reminder. In Islamic mysticism (Sufism), *dhikr* as both remembrance and reminder centers as well on meditative practices, including breathing, reciting over and over certain phrases (called *dhikr*s), and sometimes dance-like movements.

According to the Qur'an the human being is born not sinful, but forgetful, caught up in cycles of acquisition and competition that obscure matters of ultimate concern, matters represented and condensed in an ultimate way in the day of reckoning or moment of truth.

THE GENEROUS QUR'ÁN

SURAS 1, 53: 1-18

SURAS 81-114

RENDERED INTO ENGLISH
WITH COMMENTARY

BY MICHAEL SELLS

1

THE OPENING

In the name of God
   the Compassionate the Caring
Praise be to God
   lord sustainer of the worlds
the Compassionate the Caring
master of the day of reckoning
5   To you we turn to worship
   and to you we turn in time of need
Guide us along the road straight
the road of those to whom you are giving
   not those with anger upon them
   not those who have lost the way

BECAUSE OF ITS ELOQUENT STATEMENT of devotion and the manner in which it pervades religious life, The Opening has been called the Islamic equivalent of the Lord's Prayer in Christianity.

The word translated "opening," *fātiḥa*, means the opening in the sense of the opening of a chapter or a story. Unlike the other early hymic Suras, The Opening occurs not at the end of the Qur'anic written text, but at the very beginning. It is the most recited of all Qur'anic Suras, not only in prayers and liturgy, but also in everyday life. After business transactions, for example, The Opening is recited by both parties as a mark of good faith and a solemn affirmation of the responsibilities affirmed by each partner.

The Opening is the only Sura in which the phrase "In the Name of God the Compassionate the Caring" does not occur before the Sura, but is actually considered part of the Sura itself. Just as that phrase is woven into the pattern of simple activities as a form of reminder so "Praise be to God" (*al-hamdu li llāh*) has become part of everyday speech. It is used after any good news or any praise, and as a response to the greeting "How are you?"

The two qualifications of God are "lord of the worlds" (the creator deity) and "master of the day of reckoning" (the deity who brings finality to all acts and all lives). The response for those hearing or reciting The Opening is to turn toward God in worship and for refuge.

The "the road straight" frequently is translated as "the straight path." The term rendered here as road, *ṣirāṭ*, would have connoted something grand to the inhabitants of the Arabian peninsula. There are many words in Arabic for paths; the Arabs of Muhammad's time traveled through the desert on barely discernible paths. By contrast, the word *ṣirāṭ* means a paved road, such as the roads of the Romans which the Arabian travelers might come across in their journeys.

53: 1-18

THE STAR

In the Name of God the Compassionate the Caring

By the star as it falls
Your companion has not lost his way nor is he
    deluded
He does not speak out of desire
This is a revelation
5   taught him by one of great power
and strength that stretched out over
while on the highest horizon—
then drew near and came down
two bows' lengths or nearer
10   He revealed to his servant what he revealed
The heart did not lie in what it saw
Will you then dispute with him his vision?

He saw it descending another time
at the lote tree of the furthest limit
15   There was the garden of sanctuary
when something came down over the
        lote tree, enfolding
His gaze did not turn aside nor go too far
He had seen the signs of his lord, great signs

THE FIRST EIGHTEEN VERSES of The Star are considered among the earliest revelations of the Qur'an and are the most explicit reference to Muhammad's prophetic vision. The Sura begins (1-12) with the divine voice swearing by the falling star that "your companion" has not gone mad or lost his way. "Your companion" is interpreted as Muhammad. His vision is also called a revelation (*wahy*) and is explicitly said to be rooted not in desire (*hawā*), which the Qur'an associates with the inspiration of the poets (Sura 26). The object of vision is never actually described. Instead, the text evokes the process of vision by tracing a movement along the highest horizon and then a descent and drawing near to the distance of "two bows' lengths." The passage ends with an affirmation of the validity of the vision: The heart of the prophet "did not lie in what he saw." This affirmation becomes a proof text for the claim among many mystics and philosophers that the locus of spiritual vision and mystical knowledge is the heart.

In a second passage (13-18), the divine voice, referring to Muhammad again in the third person, describes another vision ("He saw it descending another time"). Here, "the lote tree of the furthest limit" is placed in or near the enigmatic "garden of sanctuary." We are told almost nothing about the tree, except that something came upon it in an enveloping manner. Of key importance is the "gaze" of the prophet, which does not "turn aside" or "go too far." This one verse became the paradigm for Islamic reflection on the proper state in contemplation. As in many evocative passages in the Qur'an, what is left unsaid is as important as what is said. Here, the power of the vision is evoked through a depiction of the gaze of the viewer, but the vision itself is never described in detail or given fixed form in a way that limits thought or imagination.

(Continued on page 47)

The Ka'aba, the spiritual axis of the Muslim world,
at the center of the Sacred Mosque in Mecca. Pilgrims
circle the Ka'ba as part of the pilgrimage rites.

When the Qur'an states "He saw it descending another time," the antecedent of the pronoun (*hu*, it/him) is unstated, and thus the referent of the "it" is not determinable from the passage. The identity of the referent became a matter of controversy, with the debate centering upon whether or not the deity can be seen in this world. Those for whom the vision of God can only occur in the afterlife tend to interpret the it/he as referring to the messenger-angel Gabriel.

81

The Overturning

In the Name of God the Compassionate the Caring

When the sun is overturned
When the stars fall away
When the mountains are moved
When the ten-month pregnant camels
    are abandoned
5   When the beasts of the wild are herded together
When the seas are boiled over
When the souls are coupled
When the girl-child buried alive
is asked what she did to deserve murder
10   When the pages are folded out
When the sky is flayed open
When Jahím is set ablaze
When the garden is brought near
Then a soul will know what it has prepared
15   I swear by the stars that slide,
stars streaming, stars that sweep along the sky
By the night as it slips away
By the morning when the fragrant air breathes
This is the word of a messenger ennobled,
20   empowered, ordained before the lord of the throne,
holding sway there, keeping trust
Your friend has not gone mad
He saw him on the horizon clear
He does not hoard for himself the unseen

(Continued on page 50)

THIS SURA OFFERS A COSMIC UNVEILING. The sky, the seas, the mountains, the normal order of life are pulled away, and the deepest secret within is revealed.

The English word *apocalypse* is derived from the Greek word for unveiling. In The Overturning, one mark of the apocalypse will be the question addressed to young girls who were buried alive. In ancient bedouin society, male children were valued more than female children. A female child could become a financial burden, and the family's honor was always vulnerable to attacks on her honor. As in other cultures, the disparity in social value led to practices such as infanticide. By placing the condemnation of this practice within the series of apocalyptic flashes, The Overturning makes it the epitome of human wrongdoing. The recompense for such extreme evil is called *Jahīm*, one of several enigmatic terms the Qur'an uses in connection with the final reckoning (for further discussion of *Jahīm*, see Sura 83 and the accompanying commentary on it).

After twelve verses marking the overturning, the Sura states that at that time each soul will know what it has prepared. By showing the ephemerality of what seems secure, the verses on cosmic unveiling attempt to reach that place within the self that is vulnerable before questions concerning ultimate value and reality. After a series of oaths, the Sura refers back to the key vision verses of Sura 53, the vision seen at the furthest limit:

Your friend has not gone mad
He saw him on the horizon clear
He does not hoard for himself the unseen

The word for "mad" (*majnūn*) literally means possessed by the *jinn* (genies), who at the time of Muhammad were

(Continued on page 51)

49

25   This is not the word of a satan
           struck with stones

Where are you going?
This is a reminder to all beings
For those who wish to walk straight
Your only will is the will of God
      lord of all beings

associated with amorous love, madness, and poetic inspiration. Thus the Qur'an is stating not only that Muhammad is not insane, but also that he is not a poet, inspired and possessed by *jinn*. Nor is he inspired by "a satan." Satans were considered a species of jinn and the Qur'an refers to "satans" or "the satan" as sources of empty ideas and egoistic inclinations. As in Sura 53 the object of the vision is unspecified. If the pronoun were translated as "him" rather than "it," the vision would refer to the angel Gabriel who brought to Muhammad the message of the Qur'an.

The Sura ends with the statement that it is a reminder (*dhikr*) to all beings, and with the question, "Where are you going?" This reminder occurs after the language of the Sura has challenged established patterns of human endeavor and human aspiration. The cosmos itself has been presented as a kind of veil, and its merely apparent solidity has been shown at a moment when that veil is torn away. The night sky and the morning air (cool, fresh, and fragrant in the desert) have been evoked as signs of a deeper reality. Only after this vision of cosmic unveiling and appeal to the signs of nature is the question about the direction of life posed.

82

THE TEARING

In the Name of God the Compassionate the Caring

When the sky is torn
When the stars are scattered
When the seas are poured forth
When the tombs are burst open
5   Then a soul will know what it has given
       and what it has held back
Oh, O human being
       what has deceived you about your generous
         lord
who created you and shaped you and made
       you right
In whatever form he willed for you, set you

But no. Rather. You deny the reckoning
10   that over you they are keeping watch
ennobled beings, writing down
knowing what it is you do

The pure of heart will be in bliss
The hard of heart will be in blazing fire
15   the day of reckoning, burning there—
they will not evade that day

What can tell you of the day of reckoning
Again, what can tell you of the day of reckoning
A day no soul has a say for another
       and the decision is at that time with God

THE TEARING BEGINS WITH another apocalyptic vision. The first four verses in Arabic are composed in a staccato rhythm with strong alliteration. The fifth and sixth verses are composed in measured cadences filled with long vowel sounds, offering a contemplative contrast to the tension and harshness of the first four verses:

> When the sky is torn
> When the stars are scattered
> When the seas are poured forth
> When the tombs are burst open
> Then a soul will know what it has given
> and what it has held back
> Oh, O human being what has deceived you about your
> generous lord

Each soul is asked what it has given and what it has held back, that is, what acts of generosity and justice has it carried out or neglected? The question occurs within an ontological reversal. The solidities of life, the sky, the stars, the seas, even the reality of death exemplified in the tombs are revealed to be ephemeral. Those acts that might seem small or passing, what the Qur'an calls later "a mote's weight good or a mote's weight wrong" (Sura 99), are revealed as having true reality.

The question is posed to the human being (*insān*). The Arabic word *insān*, used for the human being or humanity, is never gender-specific. Translations that use the word "man" evoke a series of male gender constructions that alter the gender balance in the text. But the Qur'anic questions are always addressed to insān, to man and woman alike. The reference to your generous lord (*rabbika al-karīm*) reinforces the earlier allusion to generosity as the matrix of ethnic value.

(Continued on page 55)

Three calligraphy styles presenting the phrase
bi smi Allāh ar-Raḥmān ar-Raḥīm
(In the name of God the Compassionate the Caring),
which precedes each sura of the Qur'an.

The end of the Sura poses the question, "what can tell you of the day of reckoning?" Throughout the early Meccan Suras, the phrase translated as "what can tell you of," or "what can tell you what" (*mā adrāka mā*) marks a term that is new or obscure to the original audience. The phrase indicates a moment of mystery. The question often is only partially answered, only to be posed anew in another Sura, with another partial answer or hint. Here the Sura speaks about this day of reckoning as a day when no soul can help any other. Each individual will answer for what he or she has done. In Arabian tribal society, crimes were viewed as communal rather than individual, and were atoned for by the family of the perpetrator through a payment or the giving of a hostage other than the perpetrator. The Qur'anic notion of an existential and unavoidable individual accountability was particularly threatening to the tribal rules of blood feud and family responsibility.

83

THE CHEATS

In the Name of God the Compassionate the Caring

Cursed are the cheats
who when their portion is measured among people
    take their full share
who when they measure the share of others,
    are frauds
Do they think they will not be raised again
5   for a momentous day
a day humankind will stand before the lord
    of all beings

But no. The book of the false hearted is in Sijjín
What can tell you of Sijjín?
A book inscribed
10   Cursed are those who call it all a lie
who deny the day of reckoning
Who would deny it
    but the oppressor hard in wrong?
When our signs are recited to him, he says
    fables of the ancients

But No. Rather. Rust on their hearts
    is what they acquire
15   No. On that day they will be veiled from their
    lord
They will burn in Jahím and its fire

(Continued on page 58)

COMMENTARY

RATHER THAN AN EVOCATION of the day of reckoning, The Cheats envisions the ultimate destiny of those who spend their lives cheating and hoarding and those who are giving and accept the reality of the day of reckoning.

The descriptions are consonant with the world of seventh-century bedouin Arabia. The punishment is fixed as the Jaḥīm, a term that means fire or raging fire that was developed by later Islamic commentaries and integrated into elaborate visions of hell that circulated the Mediterranean world in late antiquity. But in the Qur'an, the discussions of the afterlife tend to be brief references, often with rare terms such as Jaḥīm. Here, because it is within a context of other proper names such as 'Illiyyīn, I have treated the word Jaḥīm as a proper name as well. Much of the effect of the early Meccan Suras is due to what is not said, to the way in which a promise or warning is given but not fixed into a temporally or spatially located heaven or hell. The result is an openness as to what the warning or promise actually means—an openness that invites each hearer or reader to meditate upon that moment in which his or her life, in its true perspective of acts of justice or injustice, generosity or meanness, is unfolded.

The promised reward is located in 'Illiyyīn. The phrase "And what can tell you of 'Illiyyīn" immediately marks the word as one that would have been mysterious to the original audience. The description is one of the royal banquet. In bedouin Arabia, people sat (and still sit) on cushions on the ground. Thus, the raised couch was associated with the august splendor of the Roman feast. Descriptions of great wines also were common in pre-Islamic poetry and many pre-Islamic poems became famous for their depictions of rare wines imported from distant places of ancient vintage. The Qur'an, which in later passages bans wine, was to make of the heavenly wine mixed with the purest spring water (an image

(Continued on page 59)

But no. The innocent will be in 'Illiyyín
What can tell you of 'Illiyyín?
20   A book inscribed
witnessed by those who are brought near
Oh the pure of heart will rejoice
on raised couches, gazing
On their faces see the radiance of joy
25   They will be given to drink a sealed, pure wine
Its seal is musk—for that let those who
      aspire, aspire—
blended with the water of Tasním
From that spring, only those brought close
      will drink
The abusers would laugh at those who kept
      the faith
30   winking to one another as they passed by
When they returned to their people
      they returned mocking
and when they saw them they said
      those people have gone astray
and *they were not appointed their keepers*

But on that day those who kept the faith
      at those who denied it will laugh
35   On couches, gazing
Were the deniers rewarded
      for what they achieved?

of unbearable beauty to the desert inhabitant) a key symbol of the paradise to come.

The end of the Sura shows the beginning of the bitterness between the young Muslim community—at first mocked and humiliated, then persecuted—and those in Mecca who rejected the messenger Muhammad and laughed at his message. As with many of the gospel parables of Jesus, the rejection of the message is met not with a command to fight back but with the warning that, in the final moment, it will be the mockers who will be mocked and the persecutors who will feel the pain.

84

THE SPLITTING

In the Name of God the Compassionate the Caring

When the heaven splits
attentive to the lord and made true
When the earth is unfolded
and pours forth what is in it and is emptied
5   attentive to the lord and made true
O human being
    toward your lord you are toiling, weary
    You will find him
Whoever is given the book on his right
will be given an easy accounting
returning to his people in joy
10   Whoever is given the book behind his back
will call out destruction
and will be swallowed in fire
He was the one happy among his friends
thinking he would always be

15   But no. Rather. His lord could see into him.
I swear by the glow of sunset
By the night and what it enfolds
By the moon when she is full
Horizon on horizon you will rise
20   And what is with them that they do not believe?
and when the Qur'an is recited for them
    do not touch their heads to the ground
    in prayer

(Continued on page 62)

THE UNVEILING OR APOCALYPSE in this Sura is both cosmic (the heaven opening up) and earth-based (the earth pouring forth and emptying). As such, the Sura resonates both with other cosmic apocalypses (Sura 82) and with the famous Sura of The Quaking (Sura 101) in which the earth also opens up to reveal its secrets. When the heaven is split and the earth unfolded, they are said to be attentive to their lord and made true (*ḥuqqat*). The expression translated here as "made true" is mysterious, and commentators have offered a variety of interpretations. The strongest interpretation, I believe, is that the heaven and earth are rectified during the day of reckoning and made attentive to the deeper reality intimated by the revelation—as if the heaven and earth carried the burden of the human condition.

The central section offers a new set of lyrical oaths ("by the glow of sunset, by the night and what it enfolds, by the moon when she is full"), followed by an assurance of unlimited possibility ("[through] horizon on horizon you will rise"). The term translated here as horizon, *ṭabaqa*, can mean any variety of station, stage, or plane. In English, the use of horizon in such figures of speech as "horizons of meaning" fits the tone and tenor of this passage most clearly.

The Sura ends with an ironic comment on those who reject the Qur'anic message of the final accounting. The prophet is told to "bring them good news of a punishing pain." The refusal to accept the final reckoning or accounting is portrayed throughout the early Meccan Suras as the fundamental obstacle to the fulfillment of any human being. It is the acceptance of a final accounting—of an ultimate and complete accountability for every act—that is the necessary precondition for the just life. In order to accept such accountability, the human needs to be constantly reminded and to accept the reminder.

(Continued on page 63)

But no, the unbelievers call it a lie
God knows what they hide
Bring them good news of a punishing pain
25   except those who keep the faith and work justice
Theirs is a recompense unending

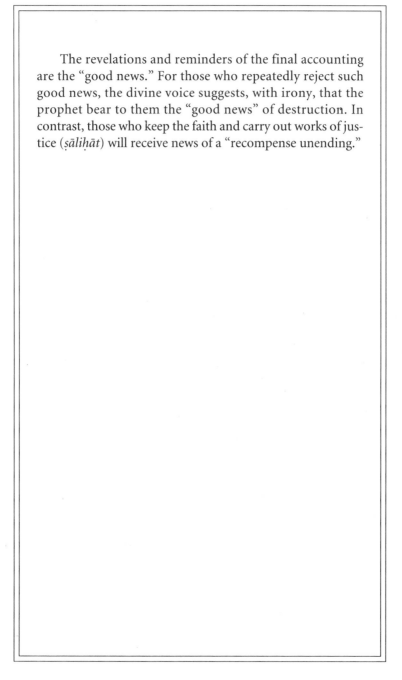

The revelations and reminders of the final accounting
are the "good news." For those who repeatedly reject such
good news, the divine voice suggests, with irony, that the
prophet bear to them the "good news" of destruction. In
contrast, those who keep the faith and carry out works of justice (*ṣāliḥāt*) will receive news of a "recompense unending."

85

THE HEAVENLY MANSIONS

In the Name of God the Compassionate the Caring

By the sky with its mansions
By the appointed day
By the witness and what is witnessed

Death to the lords of the pit
5   and its stoked fire
as they took their positions above it there
What they did to the faithful
    they are the witness to it
What did they condemn them for—
    keeping faith in God almighty, worthy
    of all praise
master of the heavens and earth?
    To all things God is witness
10   As for those who put to the trial
    the men of faith and the women of faith
    remorseless for the wrong they did—
    for them is the pain of Jahannam and the
        pain of the burning
And as for those who kept the faith and worked
    justice—for them are gardens with rivers
        flowing underground
That is the triumph supreme

(Continued on page 66)

IN THE NIGHT SKY OF THE DESERT, without lights, trees, or clouds to obscure them, the stars take on an overwhelming presence. The stars were guides for the bedouin who used them to navigate the trackless desert. They were also signs for both bedouin and agriculturists as they looked to the stars as portents of life-giving rain. The stars were organized into various systems of constellations, predictions, and foretelling the weather; one system was based on the "heavenly mansions" (*burūj*) of the Zodiac.

The reference to a people who guarded a ditch and fire, persecuted those who kept the faith, and refused to admit their wrong is obscure. Some commentators relate it to a battle between the South Yemenite Jewish king Dhū Nuwās and the Christian empire, in which the right believers were thrown into a fiery ditch. Others suggest it may be a reference to the afterlife. But whatever the specific allusion, the general message is the same: those who cause harm and then refuse to admit their wrong and atone for it will, on the "day of awe," face defeat. They will face burning and Jahannam, a term for final punishment that is cognate to the Biblical Gehenna and related to the Qur'anic Jahīm. Those who keep the faith and carry out just works will find themselves rewarded with gardens with rivers flowing underground.

The imagery is clearly based on the life of the inhabitants of Arabia, where gardens were found in oases fed by underground rivers. At the center of an oasis is the spring where the underground river opens out and flows over, a symbol for life and peace in the desert. To anyone who has ever walked into an oasis from the desert, the reference is clear. To those who have not it must be imagined: after insufferable heat, dust, and glare, the air suddenly becomes fragrant with blossoms and fruit. The sounds of birds and the rippling of

(Continued on page 67)

Unendurable is the fury of your lord
It is he who brings the beginning and brings
    the return
He is the all-forgiving, the one who holds dear
15   lord of the throne of glory
who brings to pass whatever he wills

Have you heard about the armies marching—
Pharoah and Thamúd?
But no. In denial are those who reject the faith
20   with God behind them, enfolding all
This is a glorious Qur'an, surely
On a tablet well preserved

streams replace the howl and lash of wind-whipped sand.

A sense of intimacy and peace is overwhelming. The glare and bleached-out environs give way to the deep, velvet red of pomegranate blossoms, the richness of grapes on the arbor, the majestic stands of date palms. And, of course, the temperature drops from the inhuman burning of the desert to what seem like never-ending waves of coolness. The entire experience of entering the oasis would have been evoked for an inhabitant of Arabia by the phrase "waters flowing underground."

The Sura ends with references to Pharoah and the tribe of Thamūd, two symbols of the arrogance of power, of those who thought their power was invulnerable, and yet whose power passed away. They did not realize, in their denial of God, that God is ever present and surrounding them even in their denial. The final verse states that the Qur'an is on a well preserved tablet (*lawḥ*)—a statement that has led to much discussion on the nature of such a tablet. The Qur'an is preserved in the divine mind or in some kind of primordial form. But how it is preserved on this primordial tablet became a major topic of discussion among philosophers, theologians, and mystics in the later centuries of Islam.

86

THE NIGHT-TRAVELING STAR

In the Name of God the Compassionate the Caring

By the night-traveling star
What can tell you of the night-traveling star?
The star that pierces
For every soul there is a guardian
5   Let the human being contemplate his creation
creation from a fluid gushing
between loins and ribs
He is able to bring him back again
on a day the deepest secrets will be opened
10   when a person will have no power of his own
      and no protector

By the sky that thunders
By the earth that splits
This is a word once and for all
not meant lightly
15   Cunningly they plot their design
With cunning I plot mine
Give those who deny a little time
      Give them a little time

INHABITANTS OF ANCIENT ARABIA contemplating the night sky often compared their watching of the stars as they faded over the horizon to a shepherd or herdsman tending his flock as it moved to and back from pasture. In pre-Islamic poetry, the "tending of the stars" became a major motive of night contemplation and meditation over lost loves, dangers of the journey, and human destiny.

The night traveler (*ṭāriq*) appeared frequently in pre-Islamic poetry. Much travel took place at night, when the weather was less severe and the stars served as guides. The arrival of one who traveled by night was a moment of mystery, anticipation, and danger. It could bring trouble. It could bring news of friends and loved ones. The star that was given the epithet "the night-traveler" (*aṭ-Ṭāriq*) was probably Venus, the star that traveled through the night to make her arrival in the morning.

The Sura ends with a reference to those who plot designs (*kayd*) against the deity, and the divine pronouncement that the deity plots with cunning in turn. The notion of a contest between the cunning of the prophets and their deity versus the cunning of the idolaters and their magic appears in Qur'anic stories of Moses and the Pharoah, of Abraham and the idolaters, and of Joseph and the women who tried to seduce him.

The idea of the deity exercising cunning was seized upon by missionaries who attempted to show the alleged crudity of the Islamic God. It is actually developed with richness and suppleness throughout the Qur'an and is an essential aspect of the Qur'anic meditation on the fact that those who do wrong and cause harm often prosper in this world, and those who are most giving and caring often suffer. Here the Qur'an suggests that the unbelievers are allowed "a little time" in which to enjoy their success. In moral terms, this delay is

(Continued on page 71)

The *shahada* or testimony of faith (*lā ilāha illa llāh muḥammadan rasūlu llāh*, there is no God but God, and Muhammad is the messenger of God) inscribed above a doorway.

seen as the ultimate trial. It is through the inability to recognize one's own mortality that one is led to a life of harming others. In theological terms, the notion of a divine cunning or design is essential to the issue known as theodicy, that is, the attempt to reconcile an all powerful, all benevolent deity with the prosperity of the unjust and the suffering of the innocent.

87

THE MOST HIGH

In the Name of God the Compassionate the Caring

Holy be the name of your lord most high
Who created then gave form
Who determined then gave guidance
Who made the meadow pasture grow
5   then turned it to a darkened flood-swept remnant

We will make you recite. You will not forget
    except what the will of God allows
He knows what is declared
    and what lies hidden
He will ease you to the life of ease
So remind them if reminder will succeed
10   Those who know awe will be brought to remember
He who is hard in wrong will turn away
He will be put to the fire
neither dying in it nor living
He who makes himself pure will flourish
15   who remembers the name of his lord and
    performs the prayer

But no. They prefer the lower life
Better is the life ultimate, the life that endures
As is set down in the scrolls of the ancients
the scrolls of Ibrahím and Músa

THE MOST HIGH CENTERS ON A repeated theme of the early Meccan Suras: the Qur'anic text and its messenger as a "reminder." The divine voice proclaims that Muhammad can only remind but not compel his listeners to heed the reminder. God is depicted here as the one who knows what is in the open and what is hidden. This notion of the deity will be developed throughout the Qur'an by the use of divine names such as the all-seeing (*al-baṣīr*), the all-hearing (*as-samī'*), the one who knows inside and out (*al-khabīr*), and the all-knowing (*al-'alīm*). The human being hides things from others and from himself. The being that knows these hidden, most intimate details, that knows ourselves better than we know ourselves, is the Qur'anic God, Allah.

Those who cannot be brought to remember their essential role and responsibility as human beings are said to prefer the lower life (*al-ḥayāt ad-dunyā*). The word for "lower" here is also the word, when used as a noun, for "world," a meaning that has led some translators to render the phrase "the life of the world." Although there may be a play on the two senses of *dunyā* here, grammatically the term cannot mean "life of the world" and I have adhered to the more immediate meaning of the term. The other problem with terms like "life of the world" or "worldly" is that the Qur'an generally does not view the world in negative terms, seeing it instead as the gift of an infinitely generous creator that, however transitory it may be, is to be cherished rather than despised.

The final verse suggests that the central message of The Most High is the same one that was revealed to Abraham (Ibrāhīm) and Moses (Mūsā).

88

THE DARKENING

In the Name of God the Compassionate the Caring

Have you heard the news of the darkening
Faces on that day cast down
toiling, worn
put to the fire
5   their only drink a hot spring boiling
their food, bitter-thorn
which cannot nourish
    or assuage the pangs of hunger

Faces on that day glowing in bliss
fulfilled with what they have done
10   within a garden raised high—
no empty words to hear—
with cold, gushing springs
on couches raised high
with goblets in a setting
15   with cushions arranged in place
saddle-cushions arrayed in rows

Look at the camel
    and how it is created
Look at the sky and how it is raised
Look at the mountains and how they are set
20   Look at the earth and how it is spread

(Continued on page 76)

THE DARKENING OFFERS A GLIMPSE of the day of reckoning, focusing more on the faces of those who experience it than the cosmic phenomena that herald it. This Sura contains the basic components of the hymnic apocalyptic passages: an evocation of the final day, an oath that summons the signs of the patterns of life and nature, a reference to the rejection of the prophet and of the Qur'an he brings, paradise in terms of a regal banquet.

The Qur'an has commonly been referred to as repetitive. From the thematic point of view, this is certainly the case. All the themes in The Darkening can be found in other Suras. Yet from the point of view of the Qur'anic experience, such a Sura is much more than repetition. Like a musical theme that is varied and then brought back to an original pattern, the central themes return in new combinations. There are subtle and important shifts in the imagery of the cosmic apocalypse, the psychological portrayal of those who experience the final revelation, the tone and perspective of the discussion of the role of the Qur'anic reminder, the interweaving of awe and intimacy, the movement between a depiction of the all-forgiving deity and the warnings to those who persist in doing harm.

The premise of the Qur'anic reminder is that the human being is by nature forgetful, and by habit and preoccupation caught up in the concerns of the world which hide the central reality of the moral imperative for generosity and justice. One form of reminder is the performance of the prayer: breaking the preoccupation of the day, ritually and regularly, to orient oneself toward the prophetic message and its author. The other form of reminder is the repetition and recitation, in ever new forms and supple shifts in nuance, of the basic message concerning the day of reckoning.

Remind them
    All you can do is be a reminder
Over them you have no power
As for him who rejects and turns away
God will bring down upon him great pain

25   To us they will return
    With us will be their accounting

Interior of mosque facing the *miḥrāb*,
the niche indicating the direction of Mecca.
Qur'anic calligraphy is prominent within the
elaborate tile work.

89

THE DAWN

In the Name of God the Compassionate the Caring

By the dawn
By the nights ten
By the odd and the even
By the night as it eases away
5   Is there not in that an oath for the thoughtful mind

Did you not see what your lord did to 'Ad—
great pillared Íram
like nothing created in this land before—
and Thamúd with its carvings in the river bed rock
10   and Pharoah of the tent pegs
who spread oppression through their lands
and compounded their corruption?

Your lord brought down upon them the lash
of pain
Your lord is in hiding and waits

15   Such is the human being that when his lord
tries him with generosity and bounty
he says: my lord has honored me
but when his lord tries him with hunger and lack
he says: my lord has treated me with disdain

(Continued on page 80)

'AD AND THAMUD WERE TWO ancient tribal leaders. Two great Arabian tribes and the civilizations they controlled were named after them. The civilization of Thamūd was associated with the ruins of an ancient city that may have been part of the great Nabataean empire whose capital was in Petra. The father of 'Ād was named Iram, and thus the civilization could be called either 'Ād or Iram.

By the time of Muhammad, 'Ād and Thamūd had become symoblic of great civilizations that had risen and fallen in times past. In the Qur'an, they become, along with the civilization of the Pharoahs, emblematic of those peoples who refused to hear the reminders of their prophets and ultimately came to ruin. Commentators have offered varied explanations for the mysterious term "Pharoah of the tent pegs," interpreting the pegs as a metaphor for the pyramids, for example, or simply as a figurative expression for great power as symbolized by an army with vast arrays of tents.

Thus, there are two strands of warning within the Qur'an. The first focuses on the ephemeral nature of human grandeur in time and the ruin that comes to civilizations that refuse to heed the words of their prophets. The second focuses on the fact that sometimes wrongdoers do seem to prosper and those who do right and follow the prophets remain oppressed. It suggests, in the face of such apparent injustice, that at the day of reckoning (a day that occurs on the boundary of time), both groups will finally see a just accountability.

The moral critique at the heart of this Sura becomes a key refrain for the moral critique within the early Meccan revelations, a critique of the human refusal to be giving, to help the orphan and the person in want. To be giving in this life is equated at the end of the Sura with making provisions for the moment of reckoning. After a summoning of the fear

(Continued on page 81)

But no. To the orphan you are ungiving
You do not demand food for those who hunger
You feed on inheritances and devour
20   You love possessions with a love consuming

Rather. When the earth is split apart, splitting,
    splitting
When the lord and the angels approach rank on
    rank arrayed
When on that day Jahannam is brought close
    then the human being will remember
    and what good will it do him that he
    remembers?
Saying: If only I had made provision for my life
25   On that day no one else will suffer his pain
No one will be held to the covenant he made but he

O soul made peaceful
return to your lord accepted and accepting
Come in among my servants
30   and in my garden, enter

and awe of this day, with the ranks of angels marching, the Sura ends with a reference to the peaceful soul (*an-nafs al-mutma'inna*). The soul at peace was to become a central symbol of the goal of religious life and moral discipline within Islam.

The Dawn ends with another example of the Qur'anic voice change. The "soul made peaceful" is invited to return to its lord, both accepted and accepting, in a state of reconciliation. Then the voice shifts to the deity referring to itself in the first person, a shift that gives a striking tone of intimacy to the final invitation:

> O soul made peaceful
> return to your lord accepted and accepting
> Come in among my servants
> and in my garden, enter

90

THE GROUND

In the Name of God the Compassionate the Caring

I swear by this ground
—you have come to dwell on this ground—
by the begetter and by the begotten,
we created the human being in hardship

5   Does he think there is no power over him
He says: look at the goods I devoured
Does he think no one sees him

Did we not endow him with eyes
lips and tongue
10   and guide him to the two high plains

And yet he did not climb the steep pass
What can tell you of the steep pass?

To free a slave
To feed the destitute on a day of hunger
15   a kinsman orphan
or a stranger out of luck in need

Be of those who keep the faith
    who counsel one another to patience
    who counsel to compassion
They are of the right

As for those who cast our signs away
    they are of the left
20   Over them a vault of fire

THE OATH AT THE BEGINNING OF The Ground evokes as a
sign the ground, area, or region (presumably the district
around Mecca, held as a sacred territory). In verse 2 it speaks
directly to the prophet and indirectly to other Meccans, in
stating, "you have come to dwell on this ground." The Arab
term rendered here as ground, *balad*, can mean both town
and countryside and there is a difference of opinion concerning the exact area designated by the term—whether it
means the town of Mecca or the territory or land on which
Mecca sits. I have chosen an English term, ground, that can
be as open in usage as the original Arabic. After invoking as
signs this special ground and the "the begetter and the begotten," the Sura turns to one of the fundamental messages
of the early Meccan period: condemnation of indifference
and callousness toward the orphaned and the poor.

The condemnation of indifference to the suffering of
others is brought back to the sign of the land in a graphic
manner. The emancipation of a slave or caring for the disinherited is portrayed as the climbing of a high pass, the steep,
narrow, treacherous ledge that rises up along the face of
desert mountains.

The Sura ends with a divine command to people to
counsel one another to patience and compassion, and with
a warning to those who deny the signs. The word for sign
(*āya*) means both a physical sign (such as the land) and also
a verse of the Qur'an. The verses of the Qur'an are both a
remembrance of signs that are present throughout the world
and themselves signs, which, like the signs of nature, point to
a deeper reality forgotten or neglected in everyday human
consciousness and endeavor.

91

THE SUN

In the Name of God the Compassionate the Caring

By the sun and her brightening
By the moon when it follows her
By the day when it displays her
By the night when it veils her
5   By the sky and what constructed her
By the earth and what shaped her
By the soul and what formed her
and revealed her debased and revealed her faithful
Whoever honors her flourishes
10   Whoever defiles her fails

The people of Thamúd called truth a lie
in their inhumanity
when they sent out their worst

The messenger of God said
God's camel mare
give her water!

They called him liar
and hamstrung her for the slaughter
15   Then their lord rumbled down upon them
for their crime and wiped them away
with no fear of what came after

THE SUN BEGINS WITH ONE of the most extended oaths of the Qur'an. The sun is portrayed surrounded by a court, in the most lyrical Qur'anic tone. The word for sun (*shams*) is grammatically feminine in Arabic and takes the grammatically feminine pronoun *hā*. By making hā the key rhyme word throughout the first part of the Sura, the Qur'anic voice creates a partial personification. In other words, a "gender figure" is produced. The "her" is never fully personified as a woman, but is always on the verge of such a personification.

The second part of the Sura evokes the civilization of Thamūd. For the people of Arabia, there were few symbols more potent than the tribe of Thamūd and the ruins of their great city that may have been part of the Nabataean culture whose capital was Petra, the "red rose city as old as time."

In both early Islamic poetry and the Qur'an, the destruction of Thamūd became a parable for the passing of civilizations. The poets attributed the passing of the civilization to the incessant work of fate/time (*dahr*), which wears down all things and thwarts human aspirations. The Qur'an attributed the destruction of Thamūd to the refusal of its people to heed the words of their prophet, a refusal that led to the destruction of other peoples before and after Thamūd as well.

In disobeying their prophet, Ṣāliḥ, the people of Thamūd slaughtered God's camel mare. Nothing was more taboo in ancient Arabia than the unjustified killing of a camel mare. The central ritual of pre-Islamic poetry was the camel sacrifice and distribution of the meat throughout the tribe. The improper slaying of a camel mare was a sacrilege or abomination of such enormity that it led to tribal wars that lasted generations.

By slaughtering God's camel mare, the people of Thamūd committed what was by both ancient tribal standards and Qur'anic standards an abomination. The depictions of the destruction of Thamūd are also eerily similar to depictions of the events of the day of reckoning and may serve as a parable for them as well.

92

THE NIGHT

In the Name of God the Compassionate the Caring

By the night when it falls
By the day when it breaks
By what has made the male and the female
You strive toward different ends.

5   As for him who shares what he has and is mindful
who affirms the right—
him we will ease to the good life

As for him who hoards what he has
thinking it makes him secure
who denies the right—
10   him we will ease to hardship
Wealth will not save him from ruin

Ours is guidance
Ours is the after and ours the before

I warn you of a fire that sears
15   One hard in wrong will burn there
a denier, one who turns away

(Continued on page 88)

THE NIGHT BEGINS WITH A divine invocation of the night and the day—two signs frequently evoked in Qur'anic oaths—and "what made the male and the female." The male and the female—like day and night or odd and even—are viewed as polarities that act as signs in the world and point back to their creator, who is beyond the polarities they represent. In Islamic thought, the deity is neither male nor female. Here the divine oath speaks of the very creation of gender distinction and places the creator explicitly beyond gender categories.

The Night goes on to offer a summary of the basic choices confronting humankind. The primary virtues are said to be the sharing of wealth, the affirming of the right (*al-ḥusnā*) in all, and the virtue rendered as mindfulness (*taqwā*). The term *taqwā* is notoriously difficult to translate. The root meaning is that of protecting oneself or being vigilant. Islamic commentators describe *taqwā* as a consistent and intense moral vigilance. I have used the terms "mindful" and "mindfulness" here as the closest actively used English approximation. "Righteous" and "Righteousness" have a certain power in the King James tradition, but it is difficult to find such terms being used without archaism or some form of irony. Indeed, the word righteous in contemporary speech is now frequently used to mean self-righteous—an indication that the word has evolved in usage and no longer can be used as effectively as it was.

The divine voice, the Qur'anic "we," announces that the deity will ease the way of the mindful to the good life and the way of the unmindful to hardship. This concept becomes central in Islamic theological discussion of the issue of divine providence and human free will. In this Sura, the concept of "easing the way" implies a slippery slope. Those who engage in certain forms of behavior find that their way is eased; they

(*Continued on page 89*)

We will spare from it
whoever keeps the faith
Who shares what he owns, making it pure
Who looks to no one to return the favor
20   Seeking only the face of his lord most high
That one will know peace of mind

find certain short-term gains that reinforce their behavior. The deity here personalizes its activity in "easing the way" to hardship for such people, bringing up an issue that was to engage Islamic psychologists and theologians. Moral psychologists would explore the way certain actions, such as exploitive accumulation of wealth, lead people into a self-validating world of comfort and reward, and deeper into the bonds of habit. Islamic theologians would explore, with brilliant subtlety, the tension between divine providence and human responsibility brought out by the notion that the deity "eases" those engaged in such activity to further entrenchment in their spiritual alienation.

93

THE MORNING HOURS

In the Name of God the Compassionate the Caring

By the morning hours
By the night when it is still
Your lord has not abandoned you
and does not hate you

What is after will be better
than what came before
5   To you the lord will be giving
You will be content

Did he not find you orphaned
    and give you shelter
Find you lost
    and guide you
Find you in hunger
    and provide for you

10   As for the orphan—
    do not oppress him
And one who asks—
    do not turn him away
And the grace of your lord—
    proclaim

MUHAMMAD WAS ORPHANED as a young boy and came under the protection of his grandfather. When his grandfather died, his uncle became his guardian. In a tribal society based on family and clan protection, the loss of his father and grandfather left Muhammad vulnerable to enemies in Mecca, particularly when he began reciting the Qur'anic messages that threatened the interests and beliefs of more powerful men.

In this short Sura, the Qur'anic emphasis on helping the orphaned and the disinherited is directly tied into a reminder (to Muhammad and to the listener in the more general sense) of the sufferings Muhammad experienced in his youth. Many commentators believe that this Sura was a consolation to Muhammad for the opposition and persecution he suffered as a prophet in the early Meccan years.

94

THE LAYING OPEN

In the Name of God the Compassionate the Caring

Did we not lay open your heart
and relieve you of the burden
that was breaking your back
Did we not honor your name

5   After the hard time
       there is the easing
After the hard time
       there is the easing

When you finish, strive again

And in your lord, aspire

THE PERSONAL TONE IS FURTHER intensified in the The Laying Open. It is read as a consolation meant to apply, in the first place, to the prophet Muhammad. The Sura begins with the divine voice speaking in the first person plural as "we." Some commentators have attempted to explain the Qur'anic "we" used for the deity as a reference to the heavenly court (God and the angels). Such an explanation is forced, however. Indeed, in one famous passage (Sura 2: 28-30), the divine "we" address(es) the angels as a group.

The Qur'anic divine "we" also has been compared to the "royal we" of European kings and queens. But the term connotes not only grandeur but also intimacy. One of the more supple qualities of early Arabic poetry was the way both the beloved and the lover could be referred to in either the singular or plural. This suppleness of reference, which allows for a wide shading of tone, mood, and feeling, has continued down to the present day; in popular music and songs, the beloved is commonly referred to in the plural.

The laying open of the heart refers to a relief from tension, as well as the preparation of the prophet to receive revelation. In later Islamic tradition, the opening of Muhammad's breast was literalized and portrayed as the first stage of his heavenly ascent. In these accounts, the angel Gabriel opens the breast of the prophet, takes out his heart, purifies it, and then replaces it. After the purification, Muhammad is taken on his heavenly ascent (*mi'rāj*). Such a tradition presents the opening of Muhammad as an almost shaman-like experience. Indeed, shamans from various traditions describe events like the extraction of the heart (bones or other interior organs) for cleansing as necessary initiations into their mystical or prophetic careers.

While many from the Islamic world read the Sura with the story of the Mi'raj in mind, almost all experience the Sura within the purely Qur'anic framework as well, with its directness and immediacy.

95

THE FIG

In the Name of God the Compassionate the Caring

By the fig and the olive
By Mount Sinai
By this ground inviolate

We created the human being
   in the highest station
5   then brought him down
     lowest of the low
except those who keep the faith
   and work justice
Theirs is a recompense unending

What can give you the lie then about
   the reckoning?

Is not God the judge most wise?

THE FIG BEGINS WITH AN OATH invoking the fig, the olive, and a precinct or ground that was viewed as sacred or inviolable. The oath gives a sketch of basic aspects of life in the desert.

In the Arabian peninsula and throughout the desert areas of North Africa and the Middle East, fig and olive trees along with the date palm are the visible symbols of life and fertility. In the dry river beds known as wādis, one can find areas where a fig, olive, or date tree can be sustained behind small rock dams that hold back the water the two or three times a year it rains.

In the time of Muhammad, townsmen and bedouin alike lived under the constant threat of tribal war. For both groups, the precinct around Mecca was a sacred territory (*haram*), an inviolable ground (*al-balad al-amīn*) where tribal war and other acts of violence were forbidden.

This short Sura characterizes the human condition as one that has been exalted and brought low. Those who hold the faith and do the right thing (*as-ṣāliḥāt*) will achieve an unlimited recompense in the final reckoning. The Sura ends with the question: What can give you the lie then about the *dīn*? Although *dīn* can mean either religion or reckoning, at this point in the Early Meccan period the term usually refers to religion as the acceptance of the reckoning. The focus at the end of this Sura is clearly on *dīn* as that moment of truth in which each human will find his or her most secret and most ultimate reality revealed with finality.

96

THE EMBRYO

In the Name of God the Compassionate the Caring

Recite in the name of your lord who created—
From an embryo created the human

Recite your lord is all-giving
who taught by the pen
5   Taught the human what he did not know before

The human being is a tyrant
He thinks his possessions make him secure
To your lord is the return of every thing

Did you see the one who stopped a servant
10   from performing his prayer?
Did you see if he was rightly guided
or commanded mindfulness?
Did you see him call lie and turn away?
Did he not know God could see?

15   But no. If he does not change
      we will seize him by the forelock
the lying, wrongful forelock
Let him call out his gang
We will call out the Zabániya
Do not follow him
      Touch your head to the earth in prayer
      Come near

THE EMBRYO IS NUMBERED among the first revelations, if not the first, given to Muhammad. The opening words of the Sura, "recite in the name of your lord," are interpreted as an announcement to Muhammad of the beginning of his prophecy. The site of the original revelation is believed to be the cave of Ḥirā', near Mecca, where Muhammad used to retire alone for meditation and devotions.

The word *'alaq*, translated here as embryo, has also been translated as blood clot. The word refers to something that clings, or more specifically to a coagulation of blood or other liquid. While the exact biological sense of the term is vague here, the larger meaning seems clear enough. The human being is created from humble beginnings—a drop of semen, a blood clot, an embryo. That a being with consciousness, with the ability to communicate and understand, developed from such a beginning is, in Qur'anic terms, yet another sign to be meditated upon. It is another indication of mystery, another indication that human beings, despite their rational ability and apparent self-sufficiency, are dependent on another force, both for further understanding and for being itself.

The reference to the pen is one of several Qur'anic metaphors involving instruments of writing and the tablets on which the writing occurs. Later Islamic authors interpreted the pen and the tablet (*lawḥ*)—Sura 85, final verse—in a variety of ways. Some considered the pen to be the divine intellect and the tablet the world soul on which the eternal, heavenly Qur'an is inscribed.

The Sura ends with a warning and an invitation. In the warning, those who engage in oppression are told that one day they will be judged, and that if they try to call out their gang of helpers, they will be met with a group of Zabāniya, believed by some to be a species of *jinn* (genies). The refer-

(Continued on page 99)

A Muslim performing the *sujūd* during ritual prayer (*ṣalāt*).

ence represents the kind of rough bedouin society in which force rules, with the deity suggesting that reliance on such gangs will not prevail in the ultimate struggle.

In the final invitation, the hearer is invited to touch the head to the ground in prayer. *Sujūd* can be translated as "bowing" or "prostration," but neither term is accurate. In Islamic ritual prayer, the worshiper bows, kneels, and then bends down until the head touches the ground. The term "bow" does not usually refer to touching the head to the ground while "prostration" suggests an abjectness lacking in the Islamic sense of prayer. I have rendered the term here in a way that portrays the physical motion clearly. Islam has a wide variety of prayer activity, much of which need not involve physical postures, but the ritual prayer (*ṣalāt*) is based on the movement of *sujūd*.

Islamic ritual prayer has been the target of polemicist and missionary criticism for its attention to physical movement. Such criticism is based on the belief that the physical is in opposition to the spiritual. Qur'anic *sujūd*, however, is based on the view that the physical movements, acts, and alignment (eventually toward Mecca) are one part of a complete physical and spiritual act. Muslims have explained the sense of peace and tranquility gained by performing the prayer in a variety of ways: comparing the movements to Yogic positions, the physical position to that of an infant in the womb, and touching the ground to an act of humility and an acknowledgment that the human is part of the world of creation.

97

DESTINY, AL-QADR

In the Name of God the Compassionate the Caring

Version 1

We sent it down on the night of destiny
And what could tell you of the night of destiny
The night of destiny is better than a thousand
　months
The angels come down, the spirit among them,
　by permission of their lord from every order
5　Peace it is until the rise of dawn

Version 2

We sent him down on the night of destiny
And what can tell you of the night of destiny
The night of destiny is better than a thousand
　months
The angels come down—with the spirit upon it
　by permission of their lord from every order
5　Peace she is until the rise of dawn

Version 3

We sent him down on the night of destiny
And what can tell you of the night of destiny
The night of destiny is better than a thousand
　months
The angels come down—the spirit upon her—
　by permission of their lord from every order
5　Peace she is until the rise of dawn

ALSO ASSOCIATED WITH MUHAMMAD'S prophecy is the short, exquisite Sura of *Qadr*. Qur'anic interpreters are divided upon whether the primary sense of *qadr* in this Sura is "destiny" or "power"; both interpretations are supported by the etymology of *qadr*.

In highly lyrical form, the night of the prophet's revelation is recalled, with the spirit (*rūḥ*) coming down during that night or upon that night. Constructed around this Sura is the ritual of the night of *qadr*, one of the last odd-numbered nights of the holy month of Ramadan. The festival of the night of *qadr* is often the time for a child's first attempt at fasting during Ramadan. It is also the occasion of a vigil during which the individual, family, or community may stay up through the night in prayer and meditation. The night of *qadr* comes at the end of a month of celebration and fasting during which the normal rhythms of day and night, eating and sleeping are transformed. This night is one of the more mystical moments of Islamic life. Its celebrants consider it a moment when the divine and human are particularly close to one another.

The Destiny also contains an acute version of the gender dynamic found throughout the Qur'an, but most often lost in translation. In this Sura, the phrase "night of destiny" is grammatically feminine, and the resultant pronouns and feminine–gendered verbal inflections are patterned throughout the Sura in a delicate balance with masculine–grammatical constructions. There is an undertone of implicit personification of the night as a woman, but that personification is never complete. The phrase "spirit within/upon her/it/them" (*rūḥu fīhā*) comes at the exact center of the Sura in terms of rhyme and sound, but the referent of the pronoun *hā* is ambiguous. Some say it refers to the angels (the spirit was among the angels), while others say it refers to the night (the

(Continued on page 103)

Interior courtyard of a religious school in Fez, Morocco
featuring Qur'anic calligraphy.

angels came down with the spirit on it—that is, the night). A third possibility opens up as well: The angels came down, while the spirit was upon or within the night. This possibility suggests the insemination of the night partially personified as female, in a manner strikingly similar to the insemination of Mary with Jesus as recounted elsewhere in the Qur'an.

Because the personification is not complete, translators do not feel justified in using the English feminine pronouns, but when the neuter is used, the gender balance—one of the most delicate aspects of both Qur'anic and Sufi discourse—is lost. Here are three English versions that show the various ways the Sura can be read.

(This Sura is discussed in more detail in the two chapters that follow the Suras, with a diagram that allows the reader to follow it while listening to its recitation by a Qur'anic reciter.)

98

THE TESTAMENT

In the Name of God the Compassionate the Caring

Those who denied the faith—
    from the peoples of the book
    or the idolators—
    could not stop calling it a lie
    until they received the testament

A messenger of God
    reciting pages that are pure

Of scriptures that are sure

Those who were given the book
    were not divided one against the other
    until they received the testament

5   And all they were commanded
    was to worship God sincerely
    affirm oneness, perform the prayer
    and give a share of what they have
    That is the religion of the sure

Those who deny the faith—
    from the peoples of the book
    or the idolators—

(Continued on page 106)

OF THE SHORT HYMNIC SURAS in the final section of the Qur'an, The Testament is one of the few ascribed to the later period of Muhammad's prophecy. This Sura contrasts with the early Meccan Suras in tone, style, and vocabulary. In the early Meccan period, the religion (*dīn*) was presented primarily in existential terms. Will human beings face their moral responsibility, embodied in the notion of a reckoning, and act accordingly through prayer, sharing wealth, and helping those in need? Or will they distract themselves with acquiring things and delude themselves into thinking their wealth will make them immortal?

By the later period of Muhammad's prophecy represented by The Testament, Muhammad had encountered skepticism and resistance from both the Arabian polytheists (*mushrikūn*) and "peoples of the book," that is, those with written scriptures named in other passages of the Qur'an as the Jews, Christians, and Sabaeans (the exact identity of whom has been a matter of controversy). Muhammad had thought that the Jews and Christians in Arabia would be the first to accept the message brought in the name of the tradition of Abraham, Moses, and Jesus. The rejection of that message by large portions of the Jewish and Christian communities in Arabia led to disappointment. In this Sura the concept of religion has become implicated in the tensions and rivalries among different named communities of belief.

The Testament is a consolation to Muhammad and to those who follow his message in the face of this disappointment. From the perspective of the history of religions this disappointment is similar to that expressed by some Christian writers in the refusal of Jews to recognize Jesus as the Messiah. As such it brings up the tension between religions that claim to be the culmination of a revelation (Christianity and then Islam), and religions that see themselves as the

(Continued on page 107)

are in Jahannam's fire
eternal there
They are the worst of creation

Those who keep the faith
and perform the prayer
they are the best of creation

As recompense for them with their lord—
gardens of Eden
waters flowing underground
eternal there forever

God be pleased in them
and they in God

That is for those who hold their lord in awe

faithful followers of the original revelation (Judaism vis-á-vis Christianity, Judaism and Christianity vis-á-vis Islam). While the Christianity exemplified by St. Paul views itself as the rightful inheritor of the original covenant between God and Abraham, the Qur'an views itself as the embodiment of the original, pure (ḥanīf) monotheism revealed in succession to Abraham, Moses, and Jesus. The implication is that the revelation of the Qur'an, as a testament, witness, or clear proof (bayyina)—was the occasion for a manifestation of divisions among the polytheists and peoples of the book, between those who accepted the Qur'an and those who did not.

99

THE QUAKING

In the Name of God the Compassionate the Caring

When the earth is shaken, quaking
When the earth bears forth her burdens
And someone says "What is with her?"
At that time she will tell her news
As her lord revealed her
At that time people will straggle forth
    to be shown what they have done
Whoever does a mote's weight good will see it
Whoever does a mote's weight wrong will see it

As opposed to the cosmic apocalypse in which the sky is ripped apart, The Quaking (*al-zalzala or al-zilzāl*) presents what might be called a chthonic apocalypse, with the earth opening up to yield her secrets. The bearing forth of these secrets is conveyed through a birth metaphor, with the earth (*al-arḍ*) in the feminine gender governing a series of feminine grammatical constructions. She bears them forth as or how (the Arabic construction here is tantalizingly elusive) her lord revealed them to her.

This implied metaphor and partial personification resonates powerfully with the metaphor of creation (in which the deity breathes into Adam the spirit of life); Muhammad's prophecy (where the spirit in a subtle undertone is depicted as inseminating the night of destiny, which is partially personified as female); and the conception of the prophet Jesus within Mary through the activity of the spirit. Thus, the implied personifications and sound figures that strengthen them bring together the three primordial moments of the Qur'an (creation, prophecy, and the day of reckoning) in undertones and intimations of an eternal moment in which the three moments fall into one another.

The ontological inversal here is most explicit. As the earth itself is shattered and gives forth its final secret, human beings will come forth in scattered groups to encounter what they have been and truly are. Whoever has done a "mote's weight good" will "see it"; that is, the person will see, in all its momentous finality, the act that might have seemed small at the time. Similarly, whoever has done a "mote's weight wrong," an act of injustice or neglect that might have seemed insignificant at the time, will see it in its ultimacy. As with many of the shortest Suras concerning the day of reckoning, the recognition of what has been done, of good or evil—a recognition occurring at a moment when nothing can be changed, evaded, or rewritten—is the core of the reckoning.

100

THE COURSERS

In the Name of God the Compassionate the Caring

By the coursers snorting
By the fire-strikers sparking
By the chargers at morning
Dust around them exploding
5   Within it the center holding

The human being is ungrateful to his lord.
To that he is witness
In love of wealth he is harsh
Does he not know
    that when the tombs are burst open
10   and what is hidden in the breasts revealed
on that day their lord knows through them

THE COURSERS EXEMPLIFIES what appears to be from the literary point of view a conflation of pre-Islamic paradigms of epic poetry and the apocalyptic imagery that circulated in the Near East during the time of Muhammad.

The coursers (al-ʿādiyāt) could be Arabian battle mares or horses of the apocalypse. The exact meaning of the opening short, staccato verses is as obscure as its imagery is unforgettable. These verses then open onto key themes of the early Meccan revelations. The human condition of ingratitude and greed is condemned. The Sura evokes the moment when what each of us conceals (even from himself) will be open to all, and most particularly to God who is given the epithet here of al-khabīr—that is, the one that knows through and into all things and all souls.

101

THE CALAMITY

In the Name of God the Compassionate the Caring

The *qári'a*
What is the *qári'a*
What can tell you of the *qári'a*
A day humankind are like moths scattered
5   And mountains are like fluffs of wool
Whoever's scales weigh heavy
His is a life that is pleasing
Whoever's scales weigh light
His mother is *háwiya*
What can tell you what she is
10   Raging fire

SURAT AL-QARI'A (the calamity, striking, or smiting) is composed in a pyramid structure. The Sura begins in a hymnic mode, with repetition of words and similar sound units. In the center it stretches out into longer verses and more elaborate images, with striking similes for the ontological inversion that occurs on the final day (a day humankind will be like scattered moths). The Sura then evokes the scales of justice in which human deeds are weighed. The ending of the Sura returns to the hymnic mode and introduces a strange term *hāwiya* which can mean "abyss" or "a woman bereft of her child." *Hāwiya* might even be a proper name here, under some interpretations. The term is transformed into a sound and gender figure through a series of feminine constructions that are metrically, syntactically, and phonologically stressed. *Hāwiya* evokes profound loss within a context of mystery. In the chapter "Hearing the Qur'an," a diagram will show how the term also carries within it key "sound figures," undertones that further heighten the sense of loss and of feminine gender.

The ending of the Sura involves a combination of powerful imagery and "semantic openness." After mention of the mysterious *hāwiya*, a question is asked, literally, "and what can tell you what she [i.e., *hāwiya*] is." This "what can tell you what" formula occurs in the Qur'an at critical moments concerning terms that are mysterious. The line that follows it here states simply, "raging fire." Many translators and commentators take this final answer to mean that the *hāwiya* is an epithet for the fire (i.e., hell). But such an interpretation does violence to the explicit language of the text. The final statement is not the definite "the raging fire" but rather the indefinite "raging fire."

In addition, there is a vital syntactical ambiguity: Does the expression "raging fire" serve as an example of something that could tell us what she/it is? Or is it in fact what she/it is? This syntactical ambiguity allows the reader or hearer to meditate indefinitely upon the meaning of *hāwiya*.

102

ACQUISITIVENESS

In the Name of God the Compassionate the Caring

Acquisitiveness turns you away
Until you reach the graves
Oh then you will know
Surely then you will know
Surely you will know with a knowledge certain
5   You will see a blazing fire
Then you will see it with an eye certain
At that time then
you will be asked about true well-being

As PART OF CULTURAL TRAINING for those about to visit bedouin Arab societies, visitors are cautioned about complementing anyone on a possession, whether an engraved metal coffee pot, a precious rug, or a fine horse. The host might well say to the guest not "thank you" but "it's yours" and insist the guest accept it.

This bedouin hospitality was a constant from pre-Islamic through Islamic times. In the pre-Islamic period it was associated with the generous hero, the *Karīm*, who was willing to share all he had with his tribe, including his camel mare. The Qur'an kept the emphasis on generosity, but transferred the ideal of the *Karīm* from tribal leader to the one God, and changed the mechanism of generosity from large tribal banquets to organized means of contributing to the poor. While denunciation of hoarding and acquisitiveness remained constant in pre-Islamic poetry and the Qur'an, the Qur'anic denunciations added a new theological twist. Those who spend their lives aquiring and hoarding possessions end up enslaved by those possessions and blinded by them to what ultimately matters.

The Qur'an repeats certain ideas in different ways and different contexts. Such repetition is part of its self-defined role as a "reminder," and it insists that those things that human beings forget are often the most simple and basic. The early Meccan Suras, for example, repeat the idea that human beings attempt to ignore their mortality through incessant acquisition and competition (*takāthur*). By acquiring things, the Quraysh of Mecca—and by extension all humans—are led to think their acquisitions will make them immortal. The Qur'anic reminders concerning acquisitiveness focus on the moment of final realization of what well-being, plentitude, or the true "good life" (*an-na'īm*) really is—a moment of reckoning when the goods one has grasped will be of no worth.

103

THE EPOCH

In the Name of God the Compassionate the Caring

By the age, the epoch
The human is always at a loss
Except those who keep the faith
    who work justice
    who counsel one another to truth
    and counsel one another to patience

THE EPOCH OFFERS A CONDENSED version of the ethos of the early Meccan revelations. There is no doctrine of original sin in Islam, no doctrine of an innate sinfulness that makes every human inherently unworthy of salvation without the saving grace of the deity. Instead, the Qur'an affirms that humankind is in a state of forgetfulness, confusion, and loss, and in need of reminder.

This Sura affirms that each human being is at a loss, except those who engage in four activities. The first activity is holding or keeping the faith (*imān*). This word is often translated as "belief," but *imān* includes not only intellectual assent to certain propositions but also engagement in just actions. These actions include 1) defending belief in the face of persecution or ridicule; 2) sharing wealth; 3) protecting those who are disinherited or in need; and 4) performing the ritual prayer, *ṣalāt*—the second activity explicitly mentioned in this Sura. The word *imān* also has connotations of being secure or protected. In other words, to keep the faith through an active witness that exposes one to persecution and danger, is, ironically, to gain refuge.

The last two items tie two primary virtues, the seeking of truth (*ḥaqq*) and patience (*ṣabr*), to the social nature of such activity, the mutual counseling and encouraging of friend to friend toward such ends.

104

THE SLANDERER

In the Name of God the Compassionate the Caring

Woe to every backbiting slanderer
Who gathers his wealth and counts it
thinking with his wealth he will never die
Nay, let him be thrown into the Hútama
And what can tell you of the Hútama
The fire of God, stoked for blazing
rising up over the hearts
covering them in vaults of flame
stretching out its pillars

IF THE EPOCH OFFERS A CONDENSED version of essential Qur'anic virtues, The Slanderer offers a condensed polemic against acquisitiveness. He who "gathers his wealth and counts it," does he think that his wealth will make him immortal? Self-delusion occurs when acquisitiveness distracts a person from acknowledging mortality. The Sura ends with an evocation of the finality of the moment of true recognition, when all that has been acquired is revealed as ephemeral, and humans face what they have made of their lives and selves.

The Sura ends its mordant criticism of acquisitiveness with a reference to those who have wasted their lives acquiring things being thrown into the *Ḥuṭama*. The Sura then asks what can tell us what this mysterious *Ḥuṭama* is. The final answer, the fire of God rising up over their hearts in vaults, is ambiguously related to the question. The vault of fire could be something that could tell us or give us a clue as to what the *Ḥuṭama* is. Or it could be what the *Ḥuṭama* is. The two possibilities are different. In the first case, the vault of fire can tell us something about the *Ḥuṭama*, but is not equated with the *Ḥuṭama*. In the second case, there is a complete equation.

This is another example of the syntactical ambiguity that appears after the Qur'anic expression "and what can tell you what" something is. Once again, the ambiguity keeps the question from being diminished by a facile or monotonic answer. The question continues to reverberate for each hearer or reader. It forces a continual meditation upon what it would be like to have wasted one's life and to realize that it is too late to change it.

However one interprets the fire—as a reified place in the afterlife or as a metaphor for the painful realization of a wasted life—the Qur'an's condemnation of acquisition has raised, and continues to raise, questions about the compatibility of Islamic faith with the more fiercely competitive aspects of free enterprise capitalism.

105

THE ELEPHANT

In the Name of God the Compassionate the Caring

Did you not see how your lord
    dealt with the people of the elephant
Did he not turn their plan astray
Did he not send against them birds of prey,
    in swarms
raining down stones of fire
5   making them like blasted fields of corn

At the time of Muhammad, Arabia was bounded by three major world empires: the Byzantine Roman empire, with its capital in Constantinople and territories in Syria; the Persian Sassanian empire which occupied much of present day Iraq; and the Ethiopian–Yemenite civilization to the south and southeast. All three had satellite Arabic tribes under their rule and influence, which served as buffers between them and the bedouin of central Arabia. All three had left traces of past grandeur in the great ruined cities the bedouin would come across in their travels. And finally, all three came into complicated relationships—sometimes friendly, sometimes not —with the bedouin who would be soon organized around the new religion of Islam.

The Elephant is believed to refer to an invasion of the Ethiopian prince Abraha aimed at controlling the trading center around Mecca—an invasion which, like that of Hannibal against the Romans, seems to have succeeded militarily at first, but ultimately to have failed. According to traditional sources, the incursion of Abraha occurred near the year of Muhammad's birth, 570 C.E.

The term translated as "birds of prey, in swarms" (*tayran ababīl*) has been debated by commentators. Some argue that, in order to reflect a more realistic vision of battle, the word *tayr* should be translated as horses, despite its primary meaning as birds of prey.

The reference to the stones rained down upon the people of the elephant is complicated by the descriptions of stones as being of *sijjīl*—a term related by some to words for writing. Others interpret it as a Persian loan word meaning rock, mud, or baked brick. Still others consider it a variant of the Qur'anic term *sijjīn*, which is equally obscure and sometimes associated with the fire of the final punishment.

106

QURAYSH

In the Name of God the Compassionate the Caring

For pact with Quraysh
Their pact secures a winter and summer journey
Let them worship the lord of this house
who nourished them against hunger
and secured them from fear

MUHAMMAD WAS FROM THE TRIBE of Quraysh which had controlled the trading center and pilgrimage site of Mecca for several generations. The precise nature of the trading practices of the Quraysh in Mecca, the extent of their caravans, and importance of their trade are subjects of controversy. Some claim that Mecca was at the heart of incense and spice routes from South Arabia and Yemen to the Roman and Persian empires, the trading routes of the ancient Arabia Felix (Prosperous Arabia) mentioned by the ancient Romans. Others argue that Mecca was at most a provincial trading center for local goods. By most accounts the tribe of Quraysh had some stake in or control of the sanctuary around Mecca, a town which also contained in its center the ancient shrine of the Ka'ba. The Ka'ba was referred to as the sacred house (*bayt*), and according to the Qur'an, was constructed by the prophet Abraham.

The referent for the word "them" in the phrase "let them worship the lord of this house" is believed to be the tribe of Quraysh. In other words, let the Quraysh worship the true lord of the *bayt:* Allah, the one God.

107

THE SMALL KINDNESS

In the Name of God the Compassionate the Caring

Do you see him who calls the reckoning a lie?
He is the one who casts the orphan away
who fails to urge the feeding of one in need
Cursed are those who perform the prayer
5   unmindful of how they pray
who make of themselves a display
but hold back the small kindness

THE SMALL KINDNESS RELATES A SERIES of activities in a way that grounds much of Islamic moral theology. The first act is rejecting or calling a lie the *dīn*, a word that can mean either the religion or the day of reckoning. Just as the word often translated as "believe" is more passive than the Qur'anic conception of holding fast to the belief or keeping the faith, so the concept of calling the reckoning (or religion) a lie is more active than standard English translations such as "unbelief." Those who reject the reckoning—which, in early Meccan revelations, is the foundation of religion—are those who abuse the orphan, who are indifferent to those suffering in their midst, and who are neglectful in performing the prayer. This neglectfulness has been interpreted in two ways by Qur'anic commentators: either as neglecting the proper timing and posture in performing the physical movements or as performing them mechanically while thinking about other things, without following through on the implications of the prayer for other aspects of life and behavior. The second interpretation is supported by the fact that the verse on prayer is followed by two verses on self-display and neglecting the small kindness.

Display, particularly of one's own acts of worship or piety, betrays a lack of true generosity. Self-display ends as a form of self-delusion, as a person ignores what the Qur'an announces will be ultimate in the evaluation of each life at the moment of reckoning: a genuine act of kindness, however small it might seem. There is a moral circle of causality implied in the Qur'anic passages on this issue. The refusal to acknowledge the moment of reckoning results in blindness to the small act of kindness. On the other hand, the true weight of that small act will be revealed on the day of reckoning to those who have carried it out and to those who have neglected it alike.

108

GIVEN FULLY

In the Name of God the Compassionate the Caring

Version 1

> To you we have given fully
> Pray to your lord
> and sacrifice
> The one who reviles you
> is the one who is cut

Version 2

> To you we have given *al-kawthar*
> Pray to your lord
> and sacrifice
> The one who reviles you
> is the one who is cut

ALTHOUGH MUHAMMAD HAD nine wives and several concubines, he did not have a surviving male heir. This short Sura is thought by Qur'anic commentators to have been revealed to Muhammad in consolation for the death of his son in infancy, his lack of a male heir, and the taunts he is reported to have endured because of it. It is not Muhammad who is the *abtar* (one cut, mutilated, deprived of posterity) but rather those who hate him.

According to the values of traditional tribal society in Arabia, a man's honor and status depended upon his patrilineal ancestors. It was vital for every man to have a son to carry on this lineage of honor. Men were named after their fathers and were called *ibn* or *bin* (son of). Frequently, after the birth of his first son, a father would be given a new name: *Abū* (father of) followed by the given name of the son. (In some cases, this Abū designation could be inherited from one's ancestors). Thus, Muhammad's uncle was called Abū Ṭālib (the father of Ṭālib). Muhammad's cousin 'Ali was then known as 'Alī bin Abī Ṭālib ('Ali the son of Abu Talib).

The Qur'an transforms radical tribal adherence to male lineage by redefining the individual and the community in ways that weaken the absolute authority of patriarchal kinship. The practice of naming children in a patrilineal manner remained, but the Islamic notion of a community (*umma*) of believers offered a strong balance to clan affiliation. Thus it becomes possible in this Sura for an orphan without male heirs to hear a divine voice saying "To you we have given fully"—a statement that by tribal standards of lineage-based honor would have been inconceivable.

The etymology of *kawthar* and its usage during Muhammad's time indicate the clear meaning of "abundance." According to early biographers of Muhammad, the prophet himself believed al-Kawthar was a place name for a river in paradise or a pond near the zenith of his heavenly ascent (*mi'rāj*). The glorious waters of al-Kawthar have become proverbial in Islam and resonate with a wider Mediterranean symbolism concerning the waters of life.

109

THOSE WHO REJECT THE FAITH

In the Name of God the Compassionate the Caring

Say: You who reject the faith
I do not worship what you worship
and you do not worship what I worship
I am not a worshipper of what you worship
You are not a worshipper of what I worship
5   A reckoning for you and a reckoning for me

THOSE WHO REJECT THE FAITH contains a series of hymnic repetitions. In arguing against religious intolerance, Muslim scholars frequently point to this Sura as a primary source. The Sura suggests that people worship different things and that the prophet should resign himself to that fact. It does not enjoin any kind of force to compel people to adopt the worship and faith of Islam. The forms of worship mentioned here in a general sense can be taken as differing religions or, ethically, in the sense of whatever one deems of ultimate value (the truth, al-ḥaqq).

The final verse simply states that there is a *dīn* for you and a *dīn* for me. *Dīn* can mean "religion," "way," or "reckoning." In first two cases, the implication seems to be that diversity of beliefs and values is acknowledged without any call for compulsion or conflict. If *dīn* is taken as final reckoning, the implication is more specific. There is no need for compulsion in values or beliefs now; each person will receive a just and final reckoning at the proper time.

110

HELP

In the Name of God the Compassionate the Caring

When the help of God arrived
and the opening
and you saw people joining the religion of God
in waves
Recite the praise of your lord
and say *God forgive*
He is the always forgiving

THE SHORT SURA HELP is thought to be from the later Medinan period of Muhammad's prophecy. After years of struggle, Muhammad found himself increasingly acknowledged and his Islamic community expanding. Some place the Sura after Muhammad's triumphal return to Mecca, whence he had been been expelled to Medina at the time of the hijra. After three battles between his Meccan opponents and his supporters based in Medina, he returned to Mecca victorious and made the pilgrimage there. This would be the "opening" (*fath*) of the city to the party of Muhammad. Others place the Sura before the return to Mecca and interpret the opening in more general terms, as the opening up of the way to vindication after years of struggle.

The passage opens with a "when" clause that is never finished—a distinctive feature of Qur'anic discourse. After reminding the prophet of his success, the Qur'an exhorts him to ask forgiveness.

By the grim standards of tribal warfare, the people of Mecca, having lost the war, expected looting, massacre, and the enslavement of the survivors. To the consternation of his adversaries and supporters alike, Muhammad not only refused to carry out mass revenge against the Meccan persecutors, he brought them into his movement and allowed many to rise to the highest levels of leadership in the Islamic community.

The phrase *istaghfir allāh* has now become part of everyday language in Arabic and is a common response to any kind of compliment. The term *istaghfir* means literally "ask forgiveness." It can also be translated more figuratively as "God forgive" or "God forbid"—that is, "God prevent me from taking credit or becoming proud and forgive me for having done so." From the point of view of Islamic psychology, the exclamation "God forgive" is used here to petition

(Continued on page 133)

The bismillāh invocation
in the form of an ostrich.

divine help in avoiding egoism before the prayer (poisoning the intention and thus the act of prayer before the fact) and also to ask forgiveness for egoism that occurs after the prayer (as self-congratulation poisons the act after the fact). In reference to Muhammad, the words would be an injunction to him against taking credit or becoming prideful after the victory.

111

PALM ROPE

In the Name of God the Compassionate the Caring

Broken be the hands of Ábu Láhab
   and may he break
His wealth and all that he acquired
   will not save him
He will be swallowed in fire
   and his spouse, the woodcarrier
5   around her neck a rope of palm

ACCORDING TO TRADITIONAL SOURCES, two of Muhammad's chief persecutors in Mecca were Abū Lahab and his wife, who urged Muhammad's expulsion from Mecca and persecuted him in a variety of ways. The name of the prophet's tormenter, Abū Lahab (Abī Lahab, in the grammatical construction that occurs in this Sura), means "the father of flame" or "the one with flame." The Sura makes use of the name to form a pun around the concept of fire.

As explained earlier, a new father was renamed "Abū so and so" after his first male child. Sometimes, however, a person could inherit an "Abū" designation or the word "Abū" could be used as a nickname for an attribute, as in the case of Abū Lahab (literally, the father of fire, but probably meaning one with a fiery temperament). Thus it is not always the case that a person named "Abū so and so" is the actual father of someone by that name. The sphinx in Egypt, for example, is referred to as Abū l-Hawl, "the father of terror" or the "terrible one."

This Sura is highly unusual in naming a specific enemy of Muhammad. During the Meccan period of his prophecy, Muhammad was constantly persecuted and harassed. After he had made the *hijra* to Medina, his forces fought three battles with his Meccan opponents and at times were on the edge of extinction. The Qur'an, particularly in its later Medinan Suras, contains numerous allusions to conflict, persecution, and struggles, but specific names are not given. It is only in the commentary tradition that these allusions are explained through historical discussion of specific battles and persons. Such discussions of Qur'anic allusions are called "occasions of revelation"; much Qur'anic commentary consisted of finding the specific occasion for each Qur'anic passage.

In contrast to many of the Qur'anic Suras asking Muhammad and his followers to show patience and assuring them that, despite the odds, they will be vindicated, this Sura offers a rare reflection of direct exasperation at the abuse suffered from a particular, named individual.

112

SINCERITY / UNITY

In the Name of God the Compassionate the Caring

Version 1

> Say he is God, one
> God forever
> Not begetting, unbegotten,
>> and having as an equal none

Version 2

> Say he is God, one
> God the refuge
> Not begetting, unbegotten,
>> and having as an equal none

Version 3

> Say he is God, one
> God the rock
> Not begetting, unbegotten,
>> and having as an equal none

THE MOST FAMOUS QUR'ANIC passage of *tawḥīd* (affirmation of divine unity) is among the shortest Suras of the Qur'an. In this passage, Allah is affirmed as one, not begetting, not begotten, and as *ṣamad*, an enigmatic term in classical Arabic. *Ṣamad* in pre-Islamic poetry meant a person whom one approached for refuge. Qur'anic commentators have stressed the notion of perdurance and indestructibility. Indeed, there is a feminine form of the word *ṣamada* that means a large rock. In the translations above I have given three versions, each attempting to bring out one aspect of the complex set of meanings this word signifies.

Significantly, this short Sura is called by the alternative name of sincerity (*ikhlāṣ*). In Islamic theology the notion of sincerity or authenticity is necessarily connected with the affirmation of unity. As mentioned earlier, in Islamic theology and mysticism, the affirmation of unity has several facets. It affirms that the deity has no partners or equals. In the moral sense, it has been interpreted as having no other aims, goals, or thoughts beyond the one reality or one deity. In other words, any other object that becomes an end in itself, a goal, is a form of false deity. In the theological sense, it can refer to the interior unity of the deity. To give the deity separate activities (seeing, hearing, knowing, willing) raises issues about the unity of God. If those attributes are eternal, then there are an eternal number of differing powers. If they are not eternal, then God can change, a notion that many Islamic philosophers, influenced by Aristotelian ideas about the impassivity of deity, found inconceivable. Finally, in many mystical theologies, unity involves not knowing or seeing anything but the one deity and—in the view of some mystical philosophers—arrival at a point where one's own existence passes away into the infinite reaches of that one God.

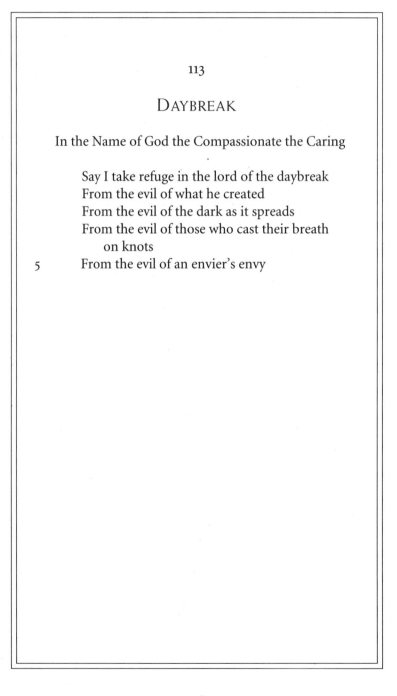

113

DAYBREAK

In the Name of God the Compassionate the Caring

Say I take refuge in the lord of the daybreak
From the evil of what he created
From the evil of the dark as it spreads
From the evil of those who cast their breath
    on knots
5   From the evil of an envier's envy

IN CONTEMPORARY ISLAMIC SOCIETIES, the phrase "I take refuge in God" (*a'ūdhu bi llāh*) is part of everyday conversation. One might pronounce the phrase upon hearing something shocking, absurd, or unbelievable, or on hearing oneself praised in a way that might lead to pride. Qur'anic reciters commonly begin each Sura with two exclamations: the obligatory "In the name of God the Compassionate, the Caring" and "I take refuge in God from Satan who is struck with stones." The second exclamation refers to an ancient ritual, within the Islamic pilgrimage or *ḥajj*, in which which pilgrims cast stones at two pillars symbolic of Satan. The casting of stones is seen as a ritual casting out of evil tendencies.

In The Daybreak, the phrase "take refuge" alludes to aspects of popular religious culture. "Those who cast their breath on knots" may refer to practitioners of witchcraft or sorcery; blowing on knots might be an attempt to "bind" the soul of an intended victim through a magic spell. The word is in the feminine form, and women were thought to have special powers in this area of popular magic. After this appeal to the fear of spells and sorcery, the first "taking refuge" Sura ends with an evocation of the evil of the envier.

In Mediterranean and Middle East societies, the power of the gaze, the look or "the eye" (*al-'ayn*) has traditionally been viewed with wariness. In folk practice, an overinvested gaze (whether of affection or malevolence) is dangerous. Infants are especially vulnerable to the danger of "the eye." Various symbols, talismans, and jewelry (including folded up pages of the Qur'an) are used to ward off its power. More is involved in such popular wisdom than "supersition," the term of dismissal used by some Western and Muslim modernists alike. In this Sura, for example, envy is seen as a palpable evil within the human condition, and such insight becomes central to Islamic moral psychology.

114

HUMANKIND

In the Name of God the Compassionate the Caring

Say I take refuge in the lord of humankind
Sovereign of humankind
God of humankind
From the evil of the whispering slinker
Whispering in the breasts of humankind
5   Of *jinn* and humankind

THE LAST SURA IS A PETITION for refuge from the evil of the whispering slinker or snub–nose. Satan was popularly portrayed as having a stubby nose and as whispering, murmuring, or insinuating. Indeed, the whisperings of pride, envy, and other faults are believed by Islamic theologians to be produced continually by the ego-self (*nafs*) and the principle of evil (Satan). Taking refuge is a form of continuous *dhikr* or remembrance. It is this constant remembrance that allows the human being to resist the suggestions of the whisperings. The syntax of the last verse (of *jinn* and humankind) is ambiguous. It could be that the whispering is *about* the *jinn* and humankind, or *by* the *jinn* and humankind.

Hearing the Qur'án

A muezzin chanting the call to prayer.

Hearing the Qur'án:
The Call to Prayer
and Six Suras

I N THE TUNISIAN TOWN of Kairouan, one of the ancient cities of Islam, the minarets and domes of the mosques are the major markers of the skyline. If one sits on the roof, as people in the Middle East and North Africa are accustomed to do, one can look out over a whitewashed city, over square roofs leading like highways through the rounded domes and past the minarets.

The minaret is a tower built for the call to prayer (adhān).[1] The name for the person who chants the call to prayer, the muezzin (mu'adhdhin), means simply one who performs the adhān or call to prayer. Because each muezzin calculates on his own the exact time of the call to prayer, and because of the distances among the mosques, the various muezzin calls begin at slightly different times. From a center city rooftop, one can hear several calls, with long, sweeping voices coming in from different directions. The call to prayer, in its distinctive chant, is one of the most memorable sounds for those who visit Islamic societies. Few who have lived there can forget waking to the sound of the predawn *adhān*, or hearing the dusk adhān in the gentle coolness of evening as the colors of the landscape soften in the waning sunlight.

The call to prayer punctuates daily life five times, drawing people out of their everyday preoccupation to matters of ultimate concern. It also contains a key Qur'anic passage and epitomizes the sound quality of Qur'anic recitation. Because of its pervasiveness in Islamic societies and its condensed manner of capturing the sound quality of the Qur'an, the call to prayer is the perfect beginning point in hearing the Qur'an. In this chapter, I have compiled a sound chart and commentary for the call to prayer and for six of the Suras discussed in this volume. Each sound chart includes a transliteration of the Arabic into English syllables, along with a word-by-word gloss that can be used to follow the recitation.

Those who perform the call to prayer are performing a kind of recitation, one of the most venerated activities within Islamic culture and civilization. In traditional Islamic cultures, children begin their primary education by learning to recite the short Suras of the Qur'an. Throughout different stages of life, people recite on various occasions and take part in recitation circles, led by a *shaykh*, or master reciter. The rules of recitation are called *tajwīd* and involve strict standards about when and how to make elisions between words, when and how to draw out certain vowel sounds or make certain sound effects with consonants. These rules are not like a musical overlay. Indeed for Muslims, the Qur'an is not "sung" and is not considered music. Instead, the literary and rhythmic qualities of the text are extensions of the inherent quality of the text itself rather than superimposed musical ornamentations.

Classical Arabic, like classical Greek or Latin, is based on a quantitative system of vowels and consonants, rather than on the accentual system used in English. Each of the three major vowels (a, i, u) can be short or long. A long vowel, transliterated in English with a macron (ā), is extended or held for twice the length of a short vowel. In Arabic metrics, a long vowel, or a short vowel followed by two consonants forms a long syllable, while a short vowel followed by a single consonant forms a short syllable. The Qur'an does not use the formal meters of Arabic poetry, which are based on combinations of long and short syllables that together form a metrical foot. Nevertheless, the Qur'an makes extraordinary use of the sounds and rhythms of Arabic.

Two of the most important effects governed by the rules of *tajwīd* are extension (*madd*) and humming or nasalization (*ghunna*). The *madd* is the elongation of long vowels at the end of verses and in other, defined situations. The ā sound is the major or tonic of Qur'anic sound figures. It is combined with key terms in a way that brings out aspects of gender, emotion, and spirit. The second effect, *ghunna*, is a nasalized hum that occurs with certain combinations of n and m or doubled n. These effects can be heard with particular significance in the Sura of Destiny. The art of *tajwīd* includes numerous other sound effects, but the sound analysis below will focus on the two most typical and important effects of *madd* and *ghunna*.

Qur'anic recitation varies from country to country and individual to individual, but there are two basic styles. The style called *tartīl* is a steady, even chant, without elaborate melodic flourishes. One would never describe it as plain, however. It has an extraordinary expressive power. The second style of Qur'anic recitation is called *tajwīd* (the same word used for the basic rules of recitation) or tajawwud. *Tajwīd* or *tajawwud* is a more elaborate style. The reciter may pause between each breath, allowing what he has recited in one full breath to echo over a meditative silence before beginning another full-breath recitation. Because the more elaborate *tajawwud* style involves dramatic use of *madd* with elaborate vocal flourishes, it is often not possible to finish an entire verse or verse section in one breath. In such cases, the reciter will back up a few words in the next breath recitation to begin from a logical break in the text, allowing for a kind of weaving of the verbal text through sound.

The enclosed CD offers recitations of the last section of the Qur'an, which can be used in connection with the sound charts of the call to prayer and the six Suras below.

Facing each sound chart is a short commentary describing the major sound figures and how they combine with meaning. The point in presenting these commentaries is not that particular sounds have inherent meaning in themselves, but that the Qur'an shapes sounds into particularly powerful combinations with meaning and feeling to create an effect in which sound and meaning are intertwined. Such combinations are not confined to a single word—such as an interjection (like the English "aha!" or "oh!") or the figure of speech known as onomatopoeia where the sound of a word echoes the effect it signifies (as in the English to "whirr")—rather, they cross the boundaries of words. They thereby create a textual harmonics of sound figures with emotional, semantic, and gendered implications.

For a preliminary sense of how these sound figures might function in the Qur'an, let us look at a different mode of speech. In the U.S. presidential race of 1956 the phrase "I like Ike" became a centerpiece of Dwight Eisenhower's campaign and one of the most successful advertising jingles in history. The linguist Roman Jakobson analyzed the phrase in detail, explaining how its success was only partly due to the rhyming. The meaning of the word "like," Jakobson argued, was transferred to Ike in an acoustical way that works beyond and beneath the explicit message. In such case a sound becomes emotive; that is, it takes on a sense of emotion, a certain emotional coloring.

Let me emphasize that the sound (in this case *ay*), has no emotional coloring in itself, but takes it on only insofar as it is placed within certain relationships. The positive feelings "ay" picks up are due to the assonance that links the "ay" sound in I, like, and Ike. The center word "like" contains both the "*ay*" of "I" and the "*ayk*" of "Ike"; in other words the sounds of "like" acoustically embrace the entire three words and lend the meaning of like to all three words. The good feelings picked up by the sound "ay" are then transferred to the nickname "Ike" in a way that works beneath the explicit, conscious message and engages the subconscious as well.

There is a skepticism in our culture shown about claims that sound patterns work in subconscious ways. The counterproof to such skepticism is found in the billions of dollars spent by advertising agencies to get just the right name for a product and right sound for a jingle. Any advertising executive can tell you that the slightest alteration in an ad's sound pattern can make or break the success of a product.[2]

In terms of value, use, and meaning in people's lives, a sacred text and an advertising jingle are at opposite edges of the spectrum. Yet the text of the Qur'an is made up of features common to all language. If sound patterns, at a very basic level, have such a powerful effect in the banal context of marketing, imagine the effect of far deeper patterns extended through a sacred text that raises questions about the meaning of life, the source of life, the end of life, and the source of knowledge. A vital feature of the Qur'an, and one of the reasons for its extraordinary resistance to translation, is its underlying sound vision. In the passages below, I will concentrate on one particular sound pattern, formed around the ā sound, that brings together emotion, meaning, and gender associations.

First I have translated the call to prayer and six suras. After each translation, you will find a transliteration and a word-by-word gloss. The gloss follows the Arabic word order, so you can follow the Arabic as it is recited. Such glosses are notations meant only to be used with the Arabic transliteration; they do not make sense according to English grammar. However, when you have read the translation, it should be possible to understand the gloss even when the word order is not grammatical in English. Facing each translation, transliteration and gloss is a set of sound notations, explaining how the Sura is recited and how the major aspects of sound within it are open to being formed into sound figures. These sound notations focus upon the development of sound figures *within* each Sura. In the final chapter of this book, I will examine the fuller significance of the sound figures as they are formed *across* the boundaries of different Suras.

CALL TO PRAYER (Sunni)
(*adhān*)

Allāhu Akbar (God is most great)	(four times)
I testify that there is no god but God	(twice)
I testify that Muhammad is the messenger of God	(twice)
Come (alive) to the prayer	(twice)
Come (alive) to flourishing	(twice)
Allāhu Akbar (God is most great)	(twice)
There is no god but God	(once)

allāhu akbar   (four times)
God is most great

ashhadu an	lā ilāha illa llāh	(twice)
I testify that (there is)	no god but God	

ashhadu anna muhammadan	rasūlu	llāh (twice)
I testify that Muhammad	is the messenger	of God

hayy	ʿala	s-salā	(twice)
come (alive)	to	the prayer	

hayy	ʿala	l-falāh	(twice)
come (alive)	to	flourishing	

allāhu akbar   (twice)
God is most great

lā ilāha illa llāh   (once)
(there is) no god but God

THE CALL TO PRAYER BEGINS WITH *Allāhu Akbar* (Allah or God is most great), a phrase that orients the worshipper toward God as the center of reality. The first two repetitions are quick and staccato. In the third and fourth repetitions, the ā sound is extended and modulated, setting the tone for the rest of the call to prayer and reflecting in amplified form a distinctive feature of all Qur'anic recitation.

After the repetitions of *Allāhu Akbar,* known as the *takbīr,* the Muezzin then recites: I testify that there is no god but God. The phrase "no god but God" is used in the Qur'an and contains, in a particularly condensed form, the Qur'anic use of sound:

lā	ilāha	illa	llāh
no	god	but	God

The entire phrase, known as the *tahlīl,* is based on the ā , l and h sounds in various combinations. The *tahlīl* is the first part of the Islamic testimony or *shahāda,* which is the first of the five pillars of Islam. The second part of the testimony then follows, repeated twice:

"I testify that Muhammad is the messenger of God."

After the completion of the *shahāda,* the Muezzin calls the faithful to prayer. *Ḥayy,* usually translated as "come," also connotes "come alive" or "live." The word for flourishing, *falāḥ,* indicates the fulfillment (in this world, the next world or both) promised in the Qur'an to those who carry out the prayer and work for justice.

The *adhān* then ends with the repetition of the *takbīr* (*allāhu akbar*) and the *tahlīl* (*lā ilāha illa llāh*). The last phrase is drawn out in a sustained, emotive cadence. It embodies the Qur'anic sound quality of *ḥuzn,* or existential sadness at the separation of humans from their source. The reminder of that separation is also a call to turn back to home.

CALL TO PRAYER (Shi'ite)
(*adhān*)

Allāhu Akbar (God is most great)   (four times)
I testify that there is no god but God   (twice)
I testify that Muhammad is the messenger of God   (twice)
Come (alive) to the prayer   (twice)
Come (alive) to flourishing   (twice)
Allāhu Akbar (God is most great)   (twice)
There is no god but God   (twice)

allāhu akbar   (four times)
God is most great

ashhadu an   lā ilāha illa llāh   (twice)
I testify that (there is)   no god but God

ashhadu anna muhammadan   rasūlu   llāh (twice)
I testify that Muhammad   is the messenger   of God

    [ashhadu   anna   'aliyyan   waliyyu llāh]
    [I testify   that   'Ali is   the Wali of God]

    [ashhadu   anna   'aliyyan   hujjatu llāh]
    [I testify   that   'Ali is   the proof of God]

hayy   'ala   s-salā   (twice)
come (alive)   to   the prayer

hayy   'ala   l-falāh   (twice)
come (alive)   to   flourishing

hayy   'alā   khayri l-'amal   (twice)
come (alive)   to   the best work

allāhu akbar   (twice)
God is most great

lā ilāha illa llāh   (twice)
(there is) no god but God

IN SHI'ITE PRACTICE, the muezzin chants the *tahlīl* (*lā ilāha illa llāh*—there is no god but God) twice in two places where the Sunni muezzin recites it once. The most distinctive part of the Shi'ite call to prayer is the formula *hayy ʿalā khayri l-ʿamal* (come alive to the best work) added after *hayy ʿala l-falāh* (come alive to flourishing).

The Shi'ite muezzin may also add two other formulas immediately after the testimony *ashhadu anna muhammadan rasūlu llāh* (I testify that Muhammad is the messenger of God):

ashhadu anna ʿaliyyan waliyyu llāh
I testify that ʿAli is the Wali of God

ashhadu anna ʿaliyyan hujjatu llāh
I testify that ʿAli is the proof of God

The word *walī* used in the first formula is one of those words that defies any single translation. It means a close friend. But it also designates someone who has been placed in a position of authority by his master (*mawlā*), a word based on the same Arabic root (w/l/y) as *walī*. God is frequently addressed as "my lord" or "our lord" (*mawlāya, mawlāna*). *Walī* then bears connations of intimate friendship, servanthood (to the *mawlā*), and authority (over whom the lord has entrusted his *walī*). In most of the Islamic world, those who have achieved special holiness are given the honorific title of *walī*, a word commonly translated as saint, but which carries all three of the meanings mentioned above. In Shi'ism, ʿAli was the first Imam, the designated leader of the community based upon the Qur'an, the revelation that was completed with the death of the prophet Muhammad. ʿAli was also God's *hujja* (proof or evidence), an honorific with an equally rich set of associations.

Muslim tradition holds that Muhammad instituted the *adhān* shortly after he arrived in Medina. Muhammad and his companions entertained a number of possible signals to mark the time for prayer, including the sound of a wooden clapper (as used by eastern Christians) or of a ram's horn, or fire as a visual cue. One companion dreamed of someone vocally calling the faithful to

Entrance to the Shaykh Luṭfullāh mosque in Isfahan, Iran.

prayer and that method was adapted. Because the *adhān* was instituted before Shi'ites believe that 'Ali's role had been manifested,
the two formulas on 'Ali are not constituted part of the adhan
proper when they are recited.

The differences in Shi'ite and Sunni *adhān*s need to be acknowledged but not exaggerated. There are also variations among
different Sunni schools of law in how many times a formula
should be chanted. In addition, the first morning *adhān* includes
the formula *aṣ-ṣalātu khayrun min an-nawm* (prayer is better than
sleep). The central focus of the *adhān*, amid these variants, remains constant. Throughout Islam, as the call to prayer is chanted,
the congregation in the mosque repeats it as they stand in readi-
ness to perform the prayer. Instead of the *ḥayy* (come alive to)
verses, they recite *lā hawla wa lā quwwata illā bi-llāh* (there is no
power and no might except with God).

1

THE OPENING

In the name of God the Compassionate the Caring
Praise be to God lord sustainer of the worlds
the Compassionate the Caring
master of the day of reckoning
5   To you we turn to worship
      and to you we turn in time of need
Guide us along the road straight
the road of those to whom you are giving
    not those with anger upon them
    not those who have lost the way

1	bi smi	llāhi	r-raḥmāni		r-raḥīm
	In the name	of God	the Compassionate		the Caring

2	al-ḥamdu	li llāhi	rabbi	l-'ālamīn
	praise	be to God	lord sustainer	of the worlds

3   ir-raḥmāni r-raḥīm
    the Compassionate the Caring

4	māliki	yawmi	d-dīn
	master	of the day	of reckoning

5	iyāka	na'budu	
	to you	we turn to worship	
		wa	iyāka	nasta'īn
		and	to you	we turn in time of need

6	ihdina	ṣ-ṣirāṭa	l-mustaqīm
	guide us	on the road	straight

7	ṣirāṭa	l-ladhīna	an'amta	'alayhim
	the road	of those	you have given	to whom
		ghayri	l-maghdūbi	'alayhim
		not those	with anger	upon them
		wa la	ḍ-ḍālīn	
		not	those who have gone astray	

Sound Cues for The Opening

The basic sound pattern of The Opening consists of an end-rhyme in *īn*, along with a long-a sound in each verse with the *īn* end-rhyme. The short verses and strong use of end-rhyme put the sura squarely in the area of the hymnic suras. Verses 9-10 are somewhat longer and break the hymnic pattern with a non-rhymic verse end (*'alayhim*) and a more prosaic style, with the same word repeated at the end of both verses. The tension caused by this interruption of the rhythm and rhyme is then released in the final verse, which is a particularly condensed example of the long-a and *īn* rhyme. The effect of returning to the basic sound pattern is hightened by the drawing out of the long-a in *ḍālīn* through the technique of *madd*, even as the *īn* is drawn out as obligatory at the end of a verse.

The elegant simplicity of the sound patterns complements the basic prayer of praise and of petition, even as the condensed quality of the sounds and short verses fits what is in fact a microcosm of basic Qur'anic beliefs in the compassionate creator, the day of reckoning, and the need for guidance.

82

THE TEARING

In the Name of God the Compassionate the Caring

When the sky is torn
When the stars are scattered
When the seas are poured forth
When the tombs are burst open
5   Then a soul will know what it has given
       and what it has held back
Oh, O human being
      what has deceived you about your generous
       lord
who created you and shaped you and made
      you right
In whatever form he willed for you, set you

But no. Rather. You deny the reckoning
10   that over you they are keeping watch
ennobled beings, writing down
knowing what it is you do

The pure of heart will be in bliss
The hard of heart will be in blazing fire
15   the day of reckoning, burning there —
they will not evade that day

What can tell you of the day of reckoning
Again, what can tell you of the day of reckoning
A day no soul has a say for another
      and the decision is at that time with God

The Tearing, Verses 1-8

bi smi	llāhi	r-raḥmāni	r-raḥīm
In the name	of God	the Compassionate	the Caring

1. idha   s-samā'u   nfaṭarat
   when   the sky   is torn

2. wa idha   l-kawākibu   ntatharat
   and when   the stars   are strewn

3. wa idha   l-biḥāru   fujjirat
   and when   the seas   are poured forth

4. wa idha   l-qubūru   bu'thirat
   and when   the tombs   are burst open

5. 'alimat   nafsun   mā qaddamat   wa akhkharat
   then will know   a soul   what it has given   and held back

6. yā ayyuha   l-insānu   mā gharraka
   oh, o   human   what has deluded

   bi rabbika l-karīm
   you from your generous lord

7. al-ladhī   khalaqaka   fa sawwāka   fa 'adalak
   who   created you   then formed you   then set you right

8. fī ayyi   ṣūratin   mā shā'a   rakkabak
   in whatever   form   he wished   he set you

Sound Cues for The Tearing, Verses 1-8

Verse Endings. Verses 1 through 5 end with a staccato assonance based on consonants and short vowels (*faṭarat, intatharat, fujjirat, buʿthirat, akhkharat*). Verse 6 changes the end-rhyme to *īm* (*karīm*) and the long vowel at the end of the verse is extended through *madd*, giving a softening and deepening effect. Verses 7 through 8 then return to the more staccato, consonant-filled ending (*ʿadalak, rakkabak*).

Major Sound Patterns. In verses 1 through 5, 7 and 8, the consonants and short vowels at the end of the verses are balanced by the long vowels in the center. In verse 1, the *ā* is extended further by *madd*. Thus one can trace two major sound patterns, with the long vowels down the middle axis of the sura and the consonant, staccato patterns at the end of the lines. In the transliteration of verses 1 through 8, the *ā*'s are in bold, while the consonant patterns and other long vowels are in italic.

Break. Verse 6 offers a complete and radical change from verses 1 through 5. The staccato patterns and consonants give way completely to a sequence of long vowels. These long vowels pick up the long vowels that were in the center of verses 1 through 4, but extend them throughout the Sura. The long vowels allow the reciter to bring out the sadness and plaintive quality of the lament given in verse 6, "Oh, O human being, what has deceived you about your generous lord." This lament contrasts in tone with the roughness of the previous verses and their evocation of the apocalypse.

Return. Verses 7 through 8 return a pattern similar to that of 1 through 5, but with a slightly different rhythm. When hearing the recitation, then, we hear three different cadences: verses 1 through 5, verse 6, and then verses 7 and 8, with verse 6 marking a shift in tone, rhyme, vowel coloration, and emotion.

Ghunna: A strong *ghunna* or nasalization occurs in verse 8 in *ṣūratin mā* ("image that"). The *n* of *ṣūratin* and the *m* of *mā* form a unit that is drawn out into a deep hum by the reciter.

The Tearing, Verses 9-19

| 9 | kallā bal | tukadhdhibūna | bi d-dīn |
| | but rather | you call a lie | the reckoning |

| 10 | wa inna | ʿalaykum | la ḥāfiẓīn |
| | but indeed | over you | are guardians |

| 11 | kirāman | | kātibīn |
| | generous | | writing |

| 12 | yaʿlamūna | mā | tafʿalūn |
| | they know | what | you do |

| 13 | inna | l-abrāra | la fī naʿīm |
| | indeed | the innocent | are in bliss |

| 14 | wa inna | l-fujjāra | la fī jaḥīm |
| | and | the wicked | are in Jaḥīm |

| 15 | yaṣlawnahā | yawm | ad-dīn |
| | burning in it | on the day | of reckoning |

| 16 | wa mā hum | ʿanhā | bi ghāʾibīn |
| | and they are not | from it | to be absent |

| 17 | wa mā | adrāka mā | yawm ud-dīn |
| | and what | can tell you what is | the day of reckoning |

| 18 | thumma mā | adrāka mā | yawm ud-dīn |
| | and then, what | can tell you what is | the day of reckoning |

| 19 | yawma | lā tamliku | nafsun li nafsin | shayʾa |
| | a day | does not have a say | a soul for another | at all |

| | wa l-amru | yawmaʿidhin | li llāh |
| | and the amr | on that day | (is, will be) with God |

Sound Cues The Tearing, Verses 9-19

Verse Endings. With the exception of verse 19, all the verses end with a long vowel and consonant, and the long vowel is elongated further through *madd*. Thus, verses 9 through 18 bring back the pattern that was an exception in the previous eight verses, that of verse 6 which ended with the word for generous (*karīm*). The two endings used are *īn* and *ūn*, which are viewed as nearly identical in Arabic poetics. The soft, extended long vowels at the end of the verses give this part of the Sura a much different flavor. They allow the reciter to extend the note of Qur'anic *huzn* or sadness.

Major Sound Patterns. In these verses, the ā sound patterns contrast, not as in verses 1 through 8 with consonant clusters, but with the ī and ū patterns that are found at the end of the verses and in various other places and are marked with italics in the sound chart. The ā sounds continue the emotive intensity they picked up from their position in the center of the verses depicting the apocalypse in verses 1 through 3, while the ī and ū patterns set up a mournful meditation on human forgetfulness and denial, and on the choices that each human can make. The final verse breaks the pattern with a series of short vowels and consantats, ending with the words "with/to God" *li llāh*. Here the ā is used in a new tone, that of a sigh, perhaps, contrasting with the emotive intensity of its use earlier in the Sura.

A Nonpersonification. The word *hā* (her/it) in some Suras clearly refers to women. In others it refers to objects with only grammatical gender. In others still (Sura 97, 99, 101) it forms a partial personification that merits translation as "her." In verses 15 and 16 above, the antecedent of *hā* is Jahīm, the mysterious word associated with the fate of the rejectors at the day of reckoning. Translating hā in this case as "her" would be unjustified, but in the Arabic it does take on a tinge of gender association, not only from its grammatical gender but also from the way the word hā has become a sound figure for a feminine being in other Suras involving the day of reckoning. While a translator might make a decision to translate some words as implicit personifications (choosing "him" or "her" over "it"), in other cases, where the choice has to be "it," the Arabic text still carries a gender undercurrent that cannot be conveyed in English.

91

The Sun

In the Name of God the Compassionate the Caring

By the sun and her brightening
By the moon when it follows her
By the day when it displays her
By the night when it veils her
5   By the sky and what constructed her
By the earth and what shaped her
By the soul and what formed her
and revealed her debased and revealed her faithful
Whoever honors her flourishes
10   Whoever defiles her fails

The people of Thamúd called truth a lie
    in their inhumanity
when they sent out their worst

The messenger of God said
    God's camel mare
    give her water!

They called him liar
    and hamstrung her for the slaughter
15   Then their lord rumbled down upon them
    for their crime and wiped them away
with no fear of what came after

The Sura of the Sun

bi smi	llāhi	r-rahmāni	r-rahīm
In the name	of God	the Compassionate	the Caring

1	wa sh-shamsi	wa	duhāhā
	by the sun	and	her brightening
2	wa l-qamari	idhā	talāhā
	by the moon	when	it follows her
3	wa n-nahāri	idhā	jallāhā
	by the day	when	it reveals her
4	wa l-layli	idhā	yaghshāhā
	by the night	when	it veils her
5	wa s-samā'i	wa mā	banāhā
	by the sky	and what	.constructed her
6	wa l-ardi	wa mā	tahāhā
	by the earth	and what	spread her out
7	wa nafsin	wa mā	sawwāhā
	by a soul	and what	shaped her
8	fa alhamahā	fujūrahā	wa taqwāhā
	and taught her	her degradation	and her faithfulness
9	qad aflaha	man	zakkāhā
	has flourished	whoever	purifies her
10	wa qad khāba	man	dassāhā
	has failed	whoever	degrades her
11	kadhdhabat	thamūdu	bi	taghwāhā
	denied	Thamúd	through	their oppression
12	idh	inba'atha		ashqāhā
	when	was sent forth		their worst

13   fa **qāla** lahum   rasūlu **llā**hi   **nāq**ata **llā**hi
     so said to them   the prophet of God: "The camel mare of God

                     wa   **suqyāhā**
                     so   give her water"

14   fa   kadhdhabūhu   fa 'aqarū**hā**
     and   they denied him   and hamstrung her

     fadamdama 'alayhim   rabbuhum   bi dhanbihim
     so poured forth upon them   their lord   for their crime

     fa sawwāhā
     and wiped them away

15   wa **lā**   ya**khā**fu   'uqba**hā**
     and did not   fear   the consequence

Sound Cues for The Sun

Verse Endings. The verses all end in the assonance/rhyme "*āhā*" and the *ā* sound is intensified by previous phrases such as *wa mā* or *idhā*. The *hā* is the grammatically feminine pronoun for "her" that is used first to refer to the sun (verses 1 through 4), the heaven and earth (verses 5, 6) and the soul (verses 7, 8, 9, 10). This ending in *hā* was also used by early Arabic poets and it allows a combination of personal references with grammatically feminine objects, facilitating a sound figure for the feminine, an intimation of personification. The intimation is so strong in this Sura that I have chosen to translate the *hā* as her.

Implicit Personification. The implicit personifications of the sun, the day and night, the heaven and earth, and the soul are reminiscent of the personification of wisdom (*hokhma*) and the portrayal of her in cosmic terms found in the biblical books of Proverbs and Ben Sira (Ecclesiasticus). The sound figure, however, does not offer a portrayal of "her" that expresses the personification as explicitly as in the biblical *hokhma*. The partial personification remains hymnic, lyrical, and implied, rather than articulated through a narrative that would portray "her" (*hā*) as a female actor in more anthropomorphic terms.

Subject and Tone Shift. In the second part of the Sura, the story of the destruction of Thamūd, the *hā* has a completely different set of referents: the people of Thamūd, the camel mare of God, and the final *hā* which is a kind of general "its". Here the *ā* builds toward an intensity in the phrase "the prophet of God said: 'God's camel mare!'" (verse 13). The phrase "God's camel mare" (*nāqata llāhi*) receives a special emphasis as it comes in the middle of the longest verse in the Sura, at the moment of greatest dramatic urgency, and its *ā* sounds allow the reciter to bring out that urgency with special resonance.

Special Effect. In the words of verse 14, "Then their lord rumbled down upon them and wiped them out," a feature of *tajwīd* called *inqilāb* is used with special effect. The word *dhanb* (crime, fault, sin) is pronounced as "*dhamb*," with a substitution of the m for n and a nasalization of the consonant cluster *mb*. This allows the weight of the consonants to sound through at a critical moment in the phrase with a sense of foreboding.

Interior of the Muhammad 'Ali mosque in Cairo, Egypt.

97

DESTINY, AL-QADR

In the Name of God the Compassionate the Caring

1	We sent him/it down on the night of destiny
2	And what could tell you of the night of destiny
3	The night of qadr is better than a thousand months
4	The angels come down—the spirit upon her—
	by permission of their lord from every order
5	Peace she is until the rise of dawn

The Sura of Destiny

bi smi	llāhi	r-raḥmāni	r-raḥīm
In the name	of God	the Compassionate	the Caring

1
Innā	anzalnā	hu	fī	laylati l-qadr
indeed	we sent down	him/it	on	the night of qadr

2
wa **mā** adrāka		**mā**	laylatu l-qadr
and what can tell you		what is	the night of qadr

3
laylatu l-qadri	khayrun	min alfi shahr
the night of destiny	is better	than a thousand months

4
tanazzalu l-malā'ikatu	wa r-rūḥu fīhā
come down the angels	and the spirit in her/it

	bi	idhni rabbihim	min kulli amr
	by	permission of their lord	from every order

5
salāmun **hiya**	ḥattā	maṭla'i l-fajr
peace she	until	the break of dawn

Sound Cues for Destiny

Verse Endings. The Sura is composed of five verses. Each verse ends with a final double consonant ending in *r*, preceded by a short vowel (*qadr, qadr, shahr, amr, fajr*). In the chart the final rhyme and assonance scheme is shown in italics.

Major Song-Vowel Pattern. The *ā* sound occurs in strategic places throughout the sura. The syllables *nā, mā, rā, lā,* and *hā* turn up as key sounds and become related to strong emotive and gender features in the Qur'an as they appear in other contexts as well.

Ghunna. An example of the untranslatability of Qur'anic sound and idiom occurs in the very first phrase of the Sura: *innā anzalnāhu.* The unit *innā* in Arabic is a combination of two words: *inn*, a particle of intensity sometimes translated (lamely) as "indeed" or "lo," and *nā*, which is the pronoun for "us." The two words are combined in a way that forms a very strong *ghunna* (nasalization) in Qur'anic recitation and the *madd* or elongation of the *ā* at the end of the *innā* increases the intensity. Then that key combination of *n* and *a* is picked up and used in the next word in various combinations: **anzalnā**. In verse 2 it is the *mā* sound which is the key. In Qur'anic recitation *m* and *n* are so closely related the *n* must be substituted for *m* under certain circumstances during the recitation. These same sound combinations of *n, a,* and *m* are found in verse 3 and open verse 4: *tanazzalu l-**malā**'ika.*

Sound Figure. The exact center of the Sura, in thematic and rhythmic terms, is the phrase *rūḥu fīhā*. The ambiguity around the referent of the pronoun *hā* (the angels, the night as the time of descent, the night as a femininely personified receiver of the revelation) puts particular power and resonance into the sound movement.

Expectation Break. The final verse, with its strong *salāmun hiya* (peace, she) and its breaking of the expectation of the expression *salāmun 'alaykum* (peace upon you), culminates the sound movements in a dramatic fashion. The implications of this breaking of expectations are explored in the final chapter of this book.

99

THE QUAKING

In the Name of God the Compassionate the Caring

When the earth is shaken, quaking
When the earth bears forth her burdens
And someone says "what is with her?"
At that time she will tell her news
5   As her lord revealed her
At that time people will straggle forth
to be shown what they have done
Whoever does a mote's weight good will see it
Whoever does a mote's weight wrong will see it

The Sura of the Quaking

bi smi	llāhi	r-rahmāni	r-rahīm
In the name	of God	the Compassionate	the Caring

1
idhā	zulzilati	l-ardu	zilzālahā
when	quakes	the earth	in her quaking

2
wa	akhrajati	l-ardu	athqālahā
and	bears forth	the earth	her burdens

3
wa	qāla	l-insānu	mā lahā
and	says	the human	"what is with her"

4
yawma'idhin	tuhaddithu	akhbārahā
on that day	she will tell	her news

5
bi'anna	rabbaka	awhā lahā
— as	her lord	revealed to her

6
yawma'idhin	yasduru	n-nāsu	ashtātan
on that day	will go forth	people	scattered

		li yuraw	a'mālahum
		to see be shown	their deeds

7
fa man	ya'mal	mithqāla dharratin	khayran	yarāh
so whoever	does	the weight of a mote	good	will see it

8
wa man	ya'mal	mithqāla dharratin	sharran	yarāh
and whoever	does	the weight of a mote	wrong	will see it

Sound Cues for The Quaking

Verse Endings. Verses 1 through 5 of The Quaking are based on a complex end rhyme in *ālahā*, with the variant *ārahā* in verse 4. The fluidity of this combination of *ā* and *h* contrasts with the sharp consonant quality of the central part of the verses: *zulzilati l-'arḍu* (verse 1), *akhrajati l-arḍu* (verse 2). These staccato combinations of consonants build up tension that is released at the end of each verse with the final *hā*.

Long-A Sound Pattern. In The Quaking the earth is caught up in a cosmic shaking. After two verses based upon *ā* and the *lahā* rhyme, the third verse takes this sound combination to a new level of intensity: *wa qāla l-insānu mā lahā*. The most cosmic moment is combined with the most intimate speech, as if a person were asking about the state of a woman's birth pangs: "and someone says 'what is with her?'" Verses 5 and 6 bring the semantic and acoustical charge of the /ā/ and the final end rhymes (*zālahā, qālahā, mā lahā, bārahā, ḥā lahā*) to the breaking point, allowing the *mā* of *mā lahā* a strong resonance as an undertone.

Verses 7 and 8, with their cosmic reversal, place the *ā* sound in the center instead of at the end. This contrast with the preceding sound patterns gives these verses a special emphasis.

Contrast. The interplay between the consonant/short-vowel staccatos and the *ā* sounds is precisely inverted in The Tearing. There, the verse endings (*infaṭarat, ntatharat, sujjirat, bu'thirat*) were staccato, while the central axis of the verses featured the *ā* (*samā', kawākib, biḥār*). In The Quaking, on the other hand, the staccato sets (*zulzilat, akhrajat*, etc.) occur in the central part of the verse, while the *ā* sounds (*zilzālahā, athqālahā*, etc.) occur at the end.

Final Effect. The last two words of the final verses, *khayran yarāh* (good will see it) and *sharran yarāh* (evil will see it), contain an effect called *idghām*, in which the final *n* of the penultimate word is elided with the following *y* and given a partial nasalization. This effect amplifies the tone of warning and foreboding with which the Sura ends.

101

The Calamity

In the Name of God the Compassionate the Caring

1	The *qári'a*
2	What is the *qári'a*
3	What can tell you of the *qári'a*
4	A day humankind are like moths scattered
5	And mountains are like fluffs of wool
6	Whoever's scales weigh heavy
7	His is a life that is pleasing
8	Whoever's scales weigh light
9	His mother is *háwiya*
10	What can tell you what she is
11	Raging fire

Sura of The Calamity

bi smi	llāhi	r-raḥmāni		r-raḥīm
In the name	of God	the Compassionate		the Caring

1   al- **qāriʿa(h)**
       the Qariʿa

2   ma l-**qāriʿa(h)**
       what is the Qariʿa

3   wa **mā** adrāka   ma   **l-qāriʿa(h)**
      what can tell you   what is the Qariʿa

4   *yawma*   *yakūnu*   *n-nāsu ka*   *l-farāshi l-mabthūth*
      (on) a day   will be   people like   moths scattered

5   *wa*   *takūnu l-jibālu*   *ka*   *l-ʿihni l-manfūsh*
      and   will be the mountains   like   wool fluffed

6   fa <u>am**mā** man</u>   thaqulat   mawāzīnuh
      as for   one   are heavy   his scales

7   fa huwa   fī   ʿīshatin   **rāḍiya(h)**
      he is   in   a life   pleased

8   wa <u>am**mā** man</u>   khaffat   mawāzīnuh
      as for   one   are light   his scales

9   fa <u>umm</u>uhu   **hāwiya(h)**
      his mother   is hāwiya

10   wa **mā**   adrāka   **mā hiya(h)**
      and what   can tell you   what she is

11   **nārun**   **ḥāmiya(h)**
      fire   raging

Sound Cues for The Calamity

Verse Endings. The dominant verse ending in The Calamity (verses 1, 2, 3, 7, 9, 10, and 11) is a complex assonance (*qāri'a, qāri'a, qāri'a, rādiya, hāwiya, mā hiya, hāmiya*). In pronouncing these sounds the reciter adds a final aspiration at the end, which is not part of the written text (h).

Long A Sound Pattern. Two of the key end rhyme words, *qāri'a* and *hāwiya*, are followed by the Qur'anic phrase "what can tell you of," which indicates these words are mysterious; indeed, they are very rare in this form in early Arabic. Both words are grammatically feminine, and the *ā* sound is tied into a grammatically feminine construction that builds toward a partial personification. The first three verses of the Sura show a progressive build-up of acoustic and emotive associations with the *mā* and the *ā*: *al-qāri'a / ma l-qāri'a / wa mā adrāka ma l-qāri'a* (the *qāri'a*, what is the *qāri'a*, what can tell you of the *qāri'a?*).

Alternate Sound Patterns. These rhythmic and hymnic sounds are interrupted in verses 4 and 5 with a very different sound cluster. The end assonance *ūth, ūsh* is based on the *ū* sound. The imagery is drawn out into more elaborate metaphors, with a rich coloration of consonants—enhanced by effects like the slight tripping sound (called *qalqala*) between the *b* and *th* of *mabthūth* in verse 5.

Expansion. Verses 6 through 9 expand into longer semantic units, with a discussion of the scales of justice. *Ghunna* is used (*fa ammā man*) in a way that recalls the beginning of the Sura of Destiny (*innā anzalnā*). In each case the nasalized m or n sounds are drawn from an intensive particle (*inn, ammā*) into the following word, creating an effect not confined to a single word. A droning sound of foreboding is heard in the verses, carried through into the first part of verse 9, *fa ummuhu*. In addition, the terms weigh heavy (*thaqulat*) and weigh light (*khaffat*) have onomatopoetic effects. One can almost hear a congealing in the movement through the three vowels of Arabic and rich consonants of *thaqulat*. And *khaffat* and surrounding words give a sense of airy aspiration, centered on the *kh* and double *f*.

Return and Sound Figure. In verses 9 through 11, we again hear the dominant *ā*, now with strong gender dynamic and parallelism among *hāwiya*, *mā hiya*, and *ḥāmiya*. Partial personification is further intimated by the word *hāwiya*, with its complex meanings (a woman bereft of her children, an abyss, with etymological associations of emptiness, air, and desire) and equally complex syntax (from "his mother is *hāwiya*" to the possibility of a curse "may his mother be *hāwiya*"). The *hā* in *hāwiya*, as it is recited, sounds forth in undertones as a kind of Arabic interjection, the Arabic equivalent of "oh!" and as the sound figure for the feminine, in its Arabic form as the pronoun for "her."

Footnotes

[1] In areas of Islamic and Christian interaction, minarets and bell towers influenced one another architecturally.

[2] R. Jakobson and Linda Waugh, *The Sound Shape of Language* (Bloomington: Indiana University Press, 1979), 177-237. See also, R. Jakobson, *Six Lectures on Sound and Meaning* (Cambridge: MIT Press, 1979); and R. Jakobson, "Linguistics and Poetics," in *Style in Language,* edited by T. A. Sebeok (Cambridge: MIT Press, 1960), 358-359. Since Jakobson's discussion, another successful commercial jingle was made of the similarly three syllabled phrase "Be like Mike."

*Sound, Spirit, and
Gender in the Qur'án*

The Ka'ba during annual pilgrimage rites.

Sound, Spirit, and Gender in the Qur'án

"God Is the All-Hearing"
(Qur'an, in 32 passages)

Spirit

I N ALEXANDRIA, EGYPT, it is a hot, humid, breezeless day. The bus is filled. People are hanging onto the steps and sitting on the roof. Inside, there is hardly room to stand, and when the bus is stopped in traffic, it is hard to breathe. The passengers fidget and struggle to be comfortable.

At some point in the two-hour trip, someone puts on a cassette of Qur'anic recitations. As the recitations play, a meditative calm begins to set in. People relax. The jockeying for space ends. The voices of those who are talking grow quieter and less strained. Others are silent, lost in thought. A sense of shared community overtakes the discomfort. What seemed at the beginning like a long ordeal is suddenly over. As the bus pulls into its destination, the spell is broken and the passengers disembark.

What was the spirit that came over these passengers? In asking such a question, I use a word, *spirit*, from everyday language that is also at the heart of the world's religious traditions. Among the common meanings of the word are: "an animating or vital principle; a supernatural being; a temper or disposition, especially when vigorous or animated; the immaterial intelligent or sentient part of a person; and an inclination, tendency, mood."[1] The English word derives from the Latin *spirare* (to blow, breathe) and the related word, *inspiration*, means, etymologically, a breathing into. There is no doubt that Qur'anic recitation is based on patterns of breath and has an effect on the breathing patterns of those who hear it. The slowing down of breathing is an essential aspect in almost all meditative traditions, and Qur'anic reciters are trained rigorously in breath control. As they recite the Qur'an in long phrases based on deep, slow exhalations, and as they leave a meditative silence during inhalation, those hearing such patterns begin to breathe more slowly and deeply.

Beyond the effects of breathing, there is a particular quality to the sound of the Qur'an that anyone familiar with it in Arabic will recognize. For centuries, Qur'anic commentators have discussed the power and beauty of this sound, what they call the *nazm* of the Qur'an, the composition, or, more loosely but perhaps more richly translated, the Qur'anic "voice." In turn, *nazm* is one of the key concepts in *i'jāz al-Qur'ān* (analysis of the inimitability of the Qur'an) which is a standard feature of Qur'anic commentary. Yet, while we have a rich history of testimonies to the power and beauty of the Qur'anic voice, few explanations have been offered for how that voice works in relationship to the sound of the Qur'an. Here I will discuss the elusive relationship of sound to meaning in the Qur'an by focusing on the Qur'anic understanding of spirit (*rūḥ*), a word that in Arabic is also related to breath. Much of the discussion of spirit in the Qur'an, in both classical commentaries and modern scholarship, is an attempt to define it as a particular being —as Gabriel, or another great angel, or yet another delimited entity. I will examine how the Qur'anic language of spirit resists reification and how it resists defining spirit as this thing or that. Rather, the Qur'an evokes the spirit in moments when the boundary between seemingly known and discreet entities is broken down.

Just as the concept of spirit is multifaceted and elusive, so the means through which the Qur'an articulates its concept of spirit are elusive. One key aspect of Qur'anic articulation is the sound figure. The sound figure is particularly subtle. It is developed within particular Suras (intratextually) and across Suras that are widely separated in the written version of the Qur'an (intertextually). The effort here is not to define "spirit" in the Qur'an; indeed, spirit transcends any particular definition or delimitation. Rather, I wish to show how the Qur'anic passages on spirit raise profound questions about the boundary moments of human life (origin, end, and source of knowledge) in a way that challenges each hearer to engage such questions through a lifetime of work and contemplation.

The Qur'anic sound figures occur in connection with three moments: prophecy, creation, and the day of reckoning. These are boundary moments, points of contact between the eternal and the temporal realms, in which the structures of language (with temporality built into them) are transformed through contact with a realm beyond temporality. In each moment, the Qur'an invokes the spirit (rūḥ).[2]

In temporal sequence the three moments are separate, but they are embedded within one another rhetorically and acoustically.[3] Passages that are separate in the written version of the Qur'an echo, allude to, or offer variations of one another in a manner that ties them together. In a tradition as recitative as that of the Qur'an, in which people hear these passages recited thousands of times, one text will provoke the reader—through a sound figure shared with a passage from a different part of the written Qur'an—to hear the second passage as an undertone. As the various passages on each boundary moment weave themselves into one another through sound figures, the three boundary moments are brought into more intimate connection. The Qur'anic references to spirit occur at center points or matrices of such connections.

185

Gender is a vital aspect of Qur'anic sound figures and the Qur'anic passages on spirit. Like all sacred texts of the classical period of religious revelations, the Qur'an was revealed in a society in which the public voice of leadership was largely male; thus, the social context of the revelation, as in the Bible or the Vedas, was largely a male domain. Yet the gender dynamic within the Qur'an contains an extraordinary balance that is constructed and modulated through sound figures. These patterns create partial personifications—of a woman giving birth, conceiving, suffering, experiencing peace, or grieving at the loss of her only child. The sound figures that create the implicit personifications also have the impact of interjections—that is, expressions of feeling, wonder, contentment, and sorrow—in which the sound itself is intertwined completely with the meaning. These sound visions occur at theologically critical moments in the Qur'an and are vital to its suppleness and beauty in the original Arabic. It may be no coincidence that spirit (*rūḥ*) is one of the few words in Arabic that can be both masculine and feminine; in the Qur'an at least, the role of spirit is both to highlight and to bring together polarities such as temporality and eternity, male and female, night and day. The Qur'an refers to the polarities as signs (*āyas*) of the deeper reality that sometimes point to a unity transcending them. The loss of such sound visions in translation is particularly damaging because of the way Islam has been perceived in stereotypes about gender and the role of women in society.

In order to show the gender and sound figures, I will consider brief passages from the early Meccan Suras as well as other passages in the Qur'an. The focus here is on sound figures essential to the intertextual evocation of spirit. Special attention is given to the Arabic sound *hā*—a sound that ties together a female pronoun; interjections of surprise, wonder, and sorrow; key rhymes; and other acoustic effects. My goal is to present enough of the original Arabic sound figures to both explore the concept of *spirit in* the Qur'an and also an essential aspect of the *spirit of* the Qur'an, that is, the distinctive manner in which the Qur'an intertwines sound and meaning.

PROPHECY

The notion of revelation contains an essential enigma. If the source of revelation is transcendent to the world and time, how can its word be communicated within time (at a particular moment in history) and language (which is structured according to temporal categories of past, present, and future)? In this sense, the language of revelation is caught in the dilemma of the boundary moment; the goal is to express the timeless, but language has ingrained patterns of temporality. Arabic verbs, for example, are either perfect (completed time) or imperfect (ongoing time), but the notion of eternity transcends such a division, and any effort to discuss the eternal inevitably temporalizes the eternal in the process. In many sacred traditions, the language depicting the moment of revelation is transformed through the encounter with the subject of timelessness.[4] In the Qur'an, a rapid shift back and forth between the perfect and the imperfect tenses destabilizes the normal mutually exclusive division between completed time and ongoing time. In addition, through its sound figures the Qur'an melds the three discreet moments of revelation, creation, and day of reckoning. The spirit is the agent of such meeting, and mention of the spirit is an indication that boundary moment transformations of language are taking place.

Spirit and prophecy are intimately linked in the most famous prophecy passages from the Qur'an. The prophetic missions of Muhammad and Jesus are specifically related to the work of the spirit. Muhammad is associated with the "spirit of transcendence," *rūḥu l-quds* (16:102), while in the case of Jesus, the spirit is said to be a support or assistance to his prophecy (2:87; 2:253; 5:110). In another passage, the spirit's relation to Jesus is put into more emphatic terms: Jesus himself is called *the spirit* (4:171). The spirit-as-support-for-Jesus passages and the Jesus-as-spirit passage echo, in sound quality and vocabulary, the Qur'anic account of the conception of Jesus.

The account of Maryam's conception of Jesus offers a unique view into the gender issues involved with the spirit. In one of the more extended passages on Maryam in the Qur'an, the angel Gabriel appears in human form and announces to Maryam that she has conceived a child. Her reaction is clearly that of a woman in the presence of a male, outside of social propriety. At first, she is worried about his intentions. Then, when he tells her she is pregnant, she is astounded and fearful. As she is about to give birth, she is in physical and emotional pain, afraid she will be a disgrace to her family. She says she wishes she never existed. At that point, she is directed to eat of the fruit of a tree dangling above her, which gives her sustenance and strength (19:16-27):

> And recall in the book Maryam,
> when she withdrew from her people to a place facing the East
>
> And veiled herself from them. We send her our spirit which took on the likeness of a fully formed human being.
>
> She said: I take refuge in the Compassionate from you. May your intentions be pure!
>
> He said: I am only a messenger from your lord, sent to bestow upon you a son without blemish.
>
> 20 She said: How can I have a son when no person has touched me and I have not been unchaste?
>
> He said: So it is! Your lord said: for me it is easy! We will make it a sign for humankind and a mercy from us—and the matter was decreed.
>
> She conceived him and withdrew to a distant place.
>
> The birth pangs drove her to the trunk of a date palm. She said: I wish I had died and were forgotten!
>
> A voice called to her from below: Grieve not. Your lord has placed a stream below you.
>
> 25 Sway the trunk of the tree toward you; ripe dates will shower down.
>
> Eat and drink and be comforted. If you meet anyone, say: I have consecrated a fast to the Compassionate and cannot speak today to any human being.
>
> She carried him forth to her people. They said: Maryam, you have brought forth a wonder!

In this passage, typical of the later period of the Qur'an, the narrative form is more elaborate; the lyric, short verses of the early period have yielded to a more prose-like composition, though still with strong acoustical effects of rhyme and assonance.

In the narrative, the spirit takes on the form of a human (*bashar*) and speaks and acts accordingly. In another account of the role of spirit in Maryam's conception, the divine voice states (21:91): "We breathed into her some of our spirit" (*nafakhnā fīhā min rūḥinā*). The exact phrasing of this statement, and especially the use of the terms *fīhā* and *rūḥ*, link this Sura to other Suras involving prophecy. In Sura 16:2, the Qur'an proclaims that God "sends down the angels, with the spirit, from his order to whichever of his servants he wills." The phrasing of this passage is vital to the Quranic accounts of spirit. It contains four sections:

1. The deity sends down angels.
2. The spirit appears in connection with the sending down of angels. The exact connection is not clear from the Arabic syntax. It could be, "He sends down the angels with the spirit," or something else.
3. The angels, with or through (*bi*) the spirit, are sent down from or with or out of (*min*) the command of God. Once again, the syntax here is open and has been the object of centuries of discussion by commentators.
4. This sending down can occur to whomever God wills.

This same fourfold phrase, with nearly identical wording and similar syntactical ambiguities, appears in verse 4 of the Sura of Destiny: "The angels and the spirit come down on it by permission of their lord from every order." In both verses there is a coming down of angels. In this descent, the exact role of the spirit is unspecified, yet crucial. The descent occurs at the order or in accordance with the order (*amr*) or by the permission (*bi idhni*) of the deity, and upon whomever the deity wills (*man yashā'*).

The first parts of these two verses are almost identical:

yunazzilu	*l-malā'ikata*	*bi*	*r-rūḥi*
he sends down	the angels	through/by/with	the spirit

tanazzalu	*l-malā'ikatu*	*wa*
they come down	the angels	while/and/as

	r-rūḥu fihā
	the spirit upon it/her

The key phrase, "the spirit upon it/her" (*ar-rūḥu fihā*), occurs at the very heart of the Sura of Destiny:

> We sent him/it down on the night of destiny
> And what could tell you of the night of destiny
> The night of destiny is better than a thousand months
> The angels come down—the spirit upon her —
>   by permission of their lord from every order
> 5 Peace she/it is until the rise of dawn.
>   (Sura of Destiny, 97)

The Sura of Destiny is based upon an only partially completed personification of the night as a woman. This personification is never made explicit in a way that would allow us the use of gendered English pronouns (she/he) without reservation. Yet the partial personification is so strong, so vital to the texture and beauty of the Sura, that to use the English "it" neuters the gender dynamic within the text. In verse 1, for example, the Arabic pronoun *hu* can be translated as either him or it. Commentators who view *hu* in a personal, gendered way interpret the referent of the pronoun as Gabriel. The divine voice, speaking as "we," announces that Gabriel has been sent down on the night of destiny. Gabriel is generally viewed as carrying the message of the Qur'an from God to Muhammad. Those commentators who view the referent as inanimate, on the other hand, interpret *it* as the Qur'an, "We sent it [the Qur'an] down" on the night of destiny.

At the most dramatic moment and rhythmic center of the Sura are three words: *rūḥu* (spirit) *fī* (in/upon) *hā* (her/it/them). This phrase is shaped by the structure of the Sura into a sound figure, with intimations of the night as a feminine personification receiving the spirit.

As we read further in Destiny, we sense stronger intimations that the Sura involves such a personification of "conception." We find a clue in the relation between verse 4 and verse 5. Verse 4 stands out as longer and more linguistically diffuse than the other verses. It contains more words and syllables than the other verses, along with a run of three subordinate clauses. By the end of these clauses, several ambiguities have been raised. What is the relation of the spirit to the coming down of the angels? Is the referent of the *hā* in *fī hā* (in it/them/her) the angels, or might it be the night? What is the relationship of this process of coming down to the divine order? Does the "coming down" occur as a result of the divine command or in harmony with it? These ambiguities, based on loose syntactical relations among key words, build up a linguistic tension. In other words, the various possibilities for interpreting the referent of *hā* leave the hearer with anticipation rather than the sense of closure that occurs at the end of an unambiguous sentence. In addition, the tight rhythms of verses 1 through 3 have temporarily been replaced in verse 4 by a series of prepositional phrases that leave the verse in a state of rhythmic as well as syntactic tension. The resulting tension puts enormous pressure on the word *fīhā* in verse 4 and high expectation on the last verse.

The final verse begins with the word *salāmun* (peace), which is usually followed in the Qur'an and in everyday Islamic greetings by the word *'alaykum* (upon you), to form the greeting, "Peace upon you" (*salāmun 'alaykum*). Expectation of such a greeting following the initial word *salāmun* is overwhelming. But, in the final verse that expectation is broken. The next word is not *'alaykum*, but *hiya* (she, it); the verse thus begins on a dramatic note of seeming familiarity, then suddenly breaks the expectations it has created and shifts to *hiya*.

The emphasis on *hiya* is compounded by a question about its grammatical antecedent, a question much discussed by classical commentators: What does *hiya* (she/it) refer to? With the gendered aspect of the pronouns highlighted throughout the Sura by sound emphasis and the implicit personification of night, the sound figure suggests that the dominant reading should be: "Peace she, until the rise of dawn." The occurrence of *hiya* also interferes with the possibility that in the previous phrase the *ha* (her/it/them) refers to the angels: "The angels came down with the spirit among them." A clear and consistent reading of the referent of *ha* as the angels would keep the *ha* from becoming a sound figure for a feminine, singular personification. However, *hiya* cannot refer grammatically to a plural (the angels), but only to a single animate being or a single object with feminine grammatical gender. Thus the appearance of *hiya* in verse 5 makes it difficult to sustain the argument that the *ha* in verse 4 refers to the angels, and thereby gives more weight to the possibility of reading the *ha* as "her."

The implied personification is also reinforced by the similarity between the word night "*layla*" and the woman's name Laylā—a name associated with one of the famous beloveds in the Arabic poetic tradition. It is true that the word *layla* is used here clearly as a word for night and not as a proper name, and that there is no direct theological connection between night and the Laylā of the poets. Nevertheless, anyone whose name sounds similar to other words knows how deeply ingrained such sound similarities are in the mind of those hearing the original name or word. The word for night, *layla*, was predisposed, through the homonymic relation to the name Laylā, to being personified, especially when other factors also suggested personification.

The final clue of such an implicit personification of the night occurs when the Sura of Destiny is read along with passages referring specifically to Maryam's conception of Jesus. In 21:91, the divine voice, speaking as "we," states of Maryam's conception of Jesus:

nafakhnā	**fīhā**	min	**rūḥinā**
We breathed	into her	(some) of	our spirit[6]

These are the exact words that occur in the Sura of Destiny, *rūḥ fīhā*, only in a different order. And in this case there is no doubt that the fīhā refers to the spirit entering the virgin Maryam and impregnating her with Jesus, the bearer of prophecy. The implicit metaphor in the Sura of Destiny is night, personified as a woman, conceiving the prophetic message through the spirit. This conception by the night of destiny is almost identical, in the language used to depict it, to the conception by Maryam of Jesus through the spirit. The personification of the night is never direct or blatant, but is heard and constructed through sound figures and undertones that make the Sura of Destiny one of the world's most beloved passages on prophecy.

CREATION

What occurred before the creation of the world? This question is a central theme in the mythic language of creation throughout human culture. However the question itself contains a contradiction, since time is part of the world. To ask what happened *before* the creation of the world is to impose a category of time as a "time before time." Thus, discussion of a time before time involves a limitless series of paradoxes. Mystical writers have used these paradoxes in powerful ways to stretch the limits of language. Philosophers have used them to critique the mythic understanding of creation. In the Qur'an, the enigma of the origin of time, of the time before time, is a second boundary moment in which the language challenges or puts into question its own structures.

References to the creation of the world are made throughout the Qur'an, usually in reference to the world as a sign of the deeper reality of the generosity of its creator. Explicit description of creation, however, focuses upon the creation of Adam. In the Qur'anic passages depicting Adam's creation, the deity first shapes (*sawwā*) the primordial human being (*insān or bashar*), then brings the form to life by breathing into it the spirit. In 15:29 and 38:71-72, the divine voice states:

| *sawwaytuhu* | *wa nafakhtu* | *fihi* | *min* |
| I shaped him it/ | and breathed | into him/it | some (of) |

| *rūhi* |
| my spirit. |

In 32:9, the divine voice uses the same formula, this time referring to itself in the third person:

sawwāhu	*wa nafakha*	*fīhi*	*min*
he/it shaped him	and breathed	into him/it	(some)

rūhihi
of his/its spirit

A key aspect of divine creativity is expressed by the Arabic word *sawwā*, a word that means to knead, to mold, to form, or to shape. Thus, just before breathing into the shape of Adam, the deity refers to his shaping of Adam with the term *sawwā*. Indeed, the term *sawwā* is intimately linked to the spirit; when something is first shaped, the spirit is then breathed into it. This term is a clue to the intertextual links among passages concerning creation. One early Meccan passage referring to the shaping of the human creature consists of the first ten verses of the Sura of the Sun. These verses are a series of oaths that announce the creative aspect of the deity through strongly gendered language. Throughout the Sura, each verse ends with the rhyme *hā*, the Arabic pronoun that can mean "her" or "it." As in Arabic poetry, which commonly used the end rhyme *hā*, the final use of *hā* allows for a gender dynamic. The *hā* can refer to female persons or to objects with grammatical gender. In verses 1 through 4, the *hā* refers to the sun. In verses 5 and 6, it can refer either to the sun or, now, the sky and earth whose creation is being discussed. In verses 7 through 10, the referent is the soul (*nafs*). Because of the way the "*hā*" is emphasized in the Sura at the end of each verse, and the way it echoes other Suras that create an implicit feminine personification, I have used the feminine pronoun "her" in the English version:

> By the sun and her brightening
> By the moon when it follows her
> By the day when it displays her
> By the night when it veils her
> 5   By the sky and what constructed her
> By the earth and what shaped her
> By the soul and what formed her (*sawwā*)
> and revealed her debased and revealed her faithful
> Whoever honors her will prosper
> 10 Whoever defiles her will find failure
>   (The Sun, 91:1-10)

This lyrical passage reflects the Quranic theme that the heavens and the earth, the day and the night, the sun and the moon are signs (*āyas*) just as the verses of the Qur'an are signs—signs of a reality that cannot be directly expressed but understood only through a sustained process of reading and interpreting. Here the reference to "a soul and what shaped her (*sawwāhā*)" repeats the technical term used in Qur'anic passages on the creation of Adam. This explicit link facilitates the more subtle links between the two passages that make use of sound patterns centered around *hā*.

The use of the rhyming hā in the Sura creates a referential suppleness. As the sound of the hā anchors the Sura, it creates a sense of a feminine-gendered presence within a set of sliding or shifting referents (the sun, the sky and the earth and/or the sun, and then the soul). The objects evoked are marks of wonder and signs of their underlying source.

Just as the spirit passage on prophecy in the Sura of Destiny showed a powerful intertextual resonance with the Qur'anic account of Maryam's conception of Jesus through the spirit, so the account of Adam's creation shows an intertextual resonance with the Maryam passage. After shaping Adam, the deity breathes into Adam some of its spirit

nafakhtu	*fīhi*	min	*rūhī*
I (Allah) breathed	into him/it	some (of)	my spirit
			(15:29, 38:72)

nafakha	*fīhi*	*min*	*rūhihi*
He (Allah) breathed	into him	(some) of	his spirit
			(32:9)

Similarly, in describing the conception of Jesus, the divine voice states (21:91): "We breathed into her some of our spirit."

nafakhnā	**fīhā**	min	**rūhinā**
we breathed	into her	(some) of	our spirit

The idea of a formed or shaped human being and the exact term used for it create another tie between the conception of Jesus and the creation of Adam. In 19:17, the divine voice proclaims that "we sent to her our spirit which appeared before her as a human being that had been shaped."

fa	arsalnā	**ilayhā**	**rūḥanā**
so	we sent	to her	our spirit

	fa	tamaththala	lahā
	which	took the appearance	before her

basharan	**sawiyyan.**
as a human	shaped

The phrase *basharan sawiyyan* (a human that had been shaped) is the exact phrase used in the story of Adam's creation to indicate the human form brought to life by the breath of the spirit. In the Maryam story, the human (*bashar*) becomes the form taken by the spirit which, in the other accounts of the conception, was breathed into Maryam. Once again, a gender dynamic is connected with the activity of the spirit. In the creation of Adam, it is the human (*insān* or *bashar*) who receives the spirit. In this passage, the pronoun used for Adam is him/it (*hu*).[6] In the other case, it is Maryam who receives the spirit that personifies itself (*tamaththala*) as a human (*bashar*). The context of social threat and Maryam's obvious discomfort make it clear that the human form of the angelic figure is male. The pronoun used for Maryam as receiver of the spirit is *hā* (her, it); there is a complementarity between the two pronouns, masculine and feminine, used for the being that receives the spirit, further heightening the issue of gender that surrounds the spirit.

These parallels—between the breathing of the spirit into the shape of Adam and the breathing of the spirit into Mary—link the two processes in a way that is never explicit, but is nevertheless robust:

fīhi (Adam) *min rūḥi*
fīhi (Adam) *min rūḥihi*
fīhā (Maryam) *min rūḥinā*
rūḥu fīhā (the Night of Destiny)

These parallels place the full weight of Qur'anic intertextuality around the key phrase in the Sura of Destiny, "the spirit in/ upon her." That intertextuality heightens the sense of implicit personification and gender interplay in the Sura. Through such intertextuality, sound figures can be heard to intimate the personification of night as feminine, conceiving the prophetic message through the spirit. In the context of such an implied personification, the night could be understood to convey peace, to conceive peace, or to be peace until the rise of dawn.

RECKONING

As the time before time (creation) is an essential enigma, so too are the end of time and the afterworld. Like creation, the day of reckoning is a boundary moment, an intersection of time and eternity that cannot be directly expressed in the temporally structured patterns of normal language. And as with creation, at the day of reckoning, spirit is the agent that brings together the eternal and the temporal:

> Someone asked about the pain that will fall
> Upon those who rejected, a pain that cannot be warded off
> From God of the ascending stairways
> **Angels ascend — and the spirit — to him**
> **on a day whose span is fifty-thousand years.**
> 5 Be patient, patience most fine
> They see it from afar
> We see it near
> A day the sky will be like molten copper
> and the mountains like fluffs of wool
> (The Stairways, 70:1-9)

The language of this passage echoes other passages on the reckoning. The mountains like fluffs of wool recall the identical image in the Sura of the Qari'a. The exact phrase "pain will fall" (adhāb wāqi') occurs in another day-of-reckoning passage:

> By the mount (Sinai)
> By the book inscribed

197

on rolls of parchment most fine
By the house brought to life
5   By the roof raised high
By the sea boiled over
The pain of your lord will fall
None can ward it off
On a day the sky will sway
and the mountains slide away
(The Mount, 52: 1-10)

The role of the spirit in the day of reckoning both echoes and inverts the role of the spirit on the night of destiny. In The Stairway (70:4), "Angels ascend — and the spirit — to him on a day whose span is fifty-thousand years." On the day of reckoning, therefore, the angels rise — in some relationship to the spirit — to him (God). On the night of destiny, the angels descend — in some relation to the spirit — to or upon the night or world. When the Sura asks what could tell us about the night of destiny, the answer is that the night of destiny is better than a thousand months. Similarly, the day of reckoning is compared to a long span of time, "a day whose span is fifty-thousand years." These parallels in imagery and meaning are further strengthened by parallels in syntax and sound:

70:4	ta'ruju	l-malā'ikatu	wa r-rūḥu	ilayhi
	there rise	the angels	and the spirit	in/upon him/it

97:4	tanazzalu	l-malā'ikatu	wa r-rūḥu	fīhā
	there descend	the angels	and the spirit	in/upon her

The coming down of the angels in connection with the activity of the spirit on the night of *qadr* is balanced by the rising of the angels in connection with spirit on the day of reckoning; in addition, the feminine indirect object (*hā*) is balanced by the masculine indirect object (*hi*). The intertwining of the two passages — one on the night of destiny, the other on the day of reckoning — intimates something undefined and perhaps undefinable hidden within the intensely lyrical imagery of daybreak in the Sura of *Qadr*. The ambiguity in both passages concerning the role of the spirit in the rise and descent of the angels creates an openness of meaning that form.

The day of reckoning and the night of destiny are brought together not only by the language of spirit but also by gendered sound figures. While in the night of destiny the sound figure intimates a woman conceiving in peace and joy, in the Sura of the Quaking, the day of reckoning is implicitly personified as a woman giving birth in crisis:

> When the earth is shaken, quaking
> When the earth bears forth her burdens
> And someone says "What is with her?"
> At that time she will tell her news
> 5   As her lord revealed her
> At that time people will straggle forth
> to be shown what they have done
> Whoever does a mote's weight good will see it
> Whoever does a mote's weight wrong will see it
>
> (The Quaking, 99)

As in the Sura of the Sun, the rhyme word is *hā* (her/it). This word is woven into a sound figure through rhetorical and acoustical structures (as shown in the sound chart for The Sun in the previous chapter). Indeed, the words spoken about the earth, "what is with her?" (*mā lahā*), are of a familiar and intimate quality that would be asked by those concerned about a woman in suffering. The depictions of earth as bearing forth her burden and telling her news create a partial and implicit image of the earth as a woman giving birth, an image that is reinforced through grammatically feminine constructions and sound figures.

After the earth bears forth her burden and tells her news, and after the quaking (which in the birth metaphor might correspond to labor), the ontological reversal that is key to the day of reckoning occurs. What seems secure and solid turns out to be ephemeral, and what seems small or insignificant is revealed as one's eternal reality and destiny.

The Sura of the Qari'a does not contain an overarching implied metaphor such as the earth giving birth. Instead, it builds with strong gender dimensions toward a moment of grief and passion. The two mysterious words in the Sura, *qāri'a* and *hāwiya*, are both feminine. And, although *hā* is not the rhyme word throughout the Sura, it is used in a particularly condensed manner to create a sound figure.

> The *qári'a*
> What is the *qári'a*
> What can tell you of the *qári'a*
> A day humankind is like moths scattered
> 5   And mountains are like fluffs of wool dyed and carded
> Whoever's scales weigh heavy
> His is a life that is pleasing
> Whoever's scales weigh light
> His mother is *háwiya*
> 10   What can tell you what she is (*mā hiya*)
> Raging fire.
>
> (The Qári'a, 101)

The *hāwiya* — a mother who has lost her child, an abyss, a fall, or desire — brings out an expression of grief. The grief and sense of loss occur with finality, but are not frozen into spatial and temporal limits. Instead, we have the refrain, "what can tell you what she is" (*mā hiya*), followed by the phrase "raging fire." Notice the syntactical ambiguity between the two verses. Is she fire, or is fire something that can tell us what she is? This ambiguity prevents a facile interpretation of the Sura and allows a continuing echo of the sound of loss, a mother's loss of her only child, or the loss of someone who realizes — at the end of a wasted life — that "his mother is *hāwiya*." The gender associations of *hā* are heightened by the rhyme and parallel to the previous *mā hiya* (what she is) in the following verse, even as the *mā hiya* reminds us of the *mā lahā* (what is with her) of the Sura of Destiny.

At this moment it is as if the language is shattered under the impact of the revelation; the word *hāwiya*, while remaining as a single word, is, in the undertones of the verse, broken into parts. As the Qur'anic reciter chants the word *hāwiya*, the syllable *hā* — which is part of the gendered sound figure in the passages on the spirit as "her" — is also heard in another key: the sound *hā* is part of several Arabic interjections of urgency, grief, or wonder. One common interjection in the Qur'an, for example, is *yā ayyuhā* ("Oh, O you"), an expression in which the long *ā* is elongated into a mournful lament through the *tajwīd* recitation. As the word *hāwiya* is recited, its first syllable sounds with lyrical intensity, gender intimation, and high emotion both as a separate unit of sound and meaning and as part of the word *hāwiya*.

THE SIGN AND THE SPIRIT

> By the dawn
> By the nights ten
> By the odd and the even
> By the night as it eases away
> 5   Is there not in that an oath for the thoughtful mind[7]
> > (Sura of the Dawn, 89:1-5)

Qur'anic oaths are another key vehicle for sound figures. Throughout the early Meccan Suras, the divine voice swears by the signs (*āyas*) of creation: by the movement of day and night, dawn and dusk, sun and moon, the stars, the zodiac; by the polarity of female and male; by the odd and the even. The Sura of The Dawn, like the Sura of Destiny, calls upon the polarity of day and night; in both Suras, that polarity is expressed in verses ending with a difficult rhyme in "r".[8]

Signs include not only signs within the world but also the verses of the Qur'an which are themselves called *āyas*. In the following oath, the dynamic of gender is not only a sign within the world but also within Qur'anic language:

> *wa l-layli idhā yaghshā*
> *wa n-nahāri idhā tajallā*
> *wa mā khalaqa dh-dhakara wa l-unthā*
>
> By the night when it falls
> By the day when it breaks
> By what (*wa mā*) has made the male and the female
> > (The Night, 92:1-3)

The relationship of sign to both gender and creation also is stressed in the story of Maryam's conception (22:91): "we breathed into her some of our spirit, and made her and her son a sign (*āya*) for all peoples." Yet, despite the critical importance of gender dynamic in the Qur'anic understanding of creation and signs, a number of popular translations follow the classical commentaries in interpreting the *mā* (what) in verse 3 above as a substitute for the Arabic pronoun *man* (who)." Some use this substitution theory to justify the English rendering of the verse as, "By Him who created the male and the female."[9]

However, the substitution theory is contradicted by the strict usage of early Arabic literature.[10] It is true that throughout the Qur'an third person reference to Allah is made through the masculine/neuter *hu*. Given that neither the Qur'an nor Islamic theology considers the one God to be differentiated sexually as male or female, however, the masculine/neuter gender construction and pronoun can be considered conventional. It is thus traditional to translate the pronoun referring to the deity in most cases as masculine. However, in this particular passage, the subject is not creation in general, but the *creation of gender*. The divine voice is swearing by that which creates the very categories of gender, of him and her. To translate that which is the creator of the male and female, and therefore necessarily transcendent to the male and the female, as "him" is to risk the loss of the transcendence of gender that is part of the Qur'anic oath. The use of "him" also loses the syntactical ambivalence between the relative pronoun (what) and the interrogative pronoun (what?) that is another aspect of the power of the oath.[11] The gender issue resurfaces in some translations of the Sura of the Sun, where the *hā* concluding each verse, which can be justifiably rendered as either "her" or "it," is translated in the masculine as "him."[12]

The loss of the Qur'anic gender dynamic in translations reinforces one of the most misleading stereotypes about Islam and the Qur'an — that the Qur'an is based on rigid, male-centered language. Yet this stereotype of a language of "he-God and he-man" is at odds not only with Islamic theology (which denies that God is male or female) but also with the intricate and beautiful gender dynamic that is a fundamental part of Qur'anic language.

That Qur'anic gender dynamic, in turn, is at the heart of the intertextuality that embeds the three boundary moments of prophecy, creation, and the reckoning one within the other — and, in so doing, transforms the temporal and sequential understanding of the three moments and intimates a sense of the eternal, in which the three moments are one.

In all three of these boundary moments, there have been implicit metaphors and intimations of personification involving women conceiving, giving birth, or bereft of their children. In each of these cases, the full significance of the sound figure can be sensed only when it is read and amplified throughout the individual Sura in which it occurs and then in relationship to the other variations in the group, each resonating within its own Sura as well.[13] Each sound combination, through its placement in a Sura, picks up a relationship to a particular meaning, emotion, or gender, and that cluster of sound, meaning, emotion, and gender then resonates with similar clusters elsewhere, turning the sound combination into a sound figure. Through the resonance of such sound figures, creation, prophecy, and reckoning — which are temporalized and separated through normal grammatical structures — are embedded within one another and detemporalized.

The partial personifications and sound figures involving spirit culminate in the phrase "peace she is" (*salāmun hiya*). The early twentieth-century scholar Richard Bell made the following elliptical comment on the Sura of Destiny: "In some ways what is here said of it [the night of *qadr*] suggests that some account of the Eve of the Nativity may have given rise to it."[14] Bell did not give his reasons for making such a speculation and his intuition was not further developed. Analysis of the sound figures in the spirit passage suggests that there is indeed connection between the night of destiny and the eve of the nativity. That connection, however, runs counter to the frequent treatment of Qur'anic themes as borrowings from Biblical traditions.

Through an intricate webbing of echoes, allusions, and resonances across the four modes of discourse (sound, meaning, emotion, gender) and across a variety of passages, the Qur'an evokes an experience of *bushrā* (bearing of good news) similar to that found in the *xaire kexaromene* (Hail, blessed one) of Luke 1:28. When we compare the various Quranic texts tied together through these resonances and hear their undertones of gender dynamic, we arrive at a sustained gender figure in which a series of partially personified female referents (the earth, the *hāwiya*, the night of *qadr*) and a related female character (Maryam) are found at the center of the experiences of prophecy, creation, and the day of reckoning. This figure is not announced on the level of surface semantics. It is certainly not "borrowed" from the Biblical text. Rather, it is created in the Qur'an through sound figures and intertextuality. The sound figures are lost when translated into a uniformly masculine or neutered English language. They are moving figures, evoked by but not confined to particular words, often stretching across verbal boundaries in a manner far more supple than the common sound-meaning figure of speech known as onomatopoesis. They can be heard through the resonances, echoes, undertones, and interstices of the Arabic text in recitation, and in such sound vision resides the distinctive Qur'anic combination of awe and intimacy.

Footnotes

[1] *Webster's Ninth New Collegiate Dictionary* (Springfield, MA: Merriam Webster, 1986).

[2] The word for spirit (*rūḥ*) occurs less than two dozen times in the Qur'an. O'Shaughnessy lists 20 instances with the Arabic citations and translations. T. O'Shaughnessy, *The Development of the Meaning of Spirit in the Koran* (Rome: Pont. Institutum Orientalium Studiorum, 1953): 13-15. Al-Bāqī's *Al-Muʿjam al-Mufahris* (Cairo: Kitāb ash-Shaʿb, n.d., p. 326, gives the same citations, only numbers them as 21 separate references, giving a separate citation to the two occurrences of the word in 17:85.

[3] Sura 32, for example, begins with a mention of Muhammad's prophecy (1-3). It moves suddenly to creation and the breathing of the spirit into the primordial human (4-9) and then, in a final sudden shift, to the day of reckoning (10-11). These are discreet verses, but even here they are brought into close connection. Through intertextual echoes even verses distant from one another in the Qur'an are interembedded.

of David Carpenter, *Revelation, History, and the Dialogue of Religions: A Study of Bhartrhari and Bonaventure* (Maryknoll, NY: Orbis Books, 1995). For the views of mystics on how the Qur'an, the book of Exodus, and the first verses of the Gospel of John shatter normal structures of language, see M. Sells, *Mystical Languages of Unsaying* (Chicago: University of Chicago Press, 1994). See also, Bernard McGinn, *The Presence of God: The Foundations of Mysticism* (New York : Crossroad, 1991), especially the chapter on the Christian mystical theologian Origen.

[5] Sura 66:12 offers a more graphic version, we breathed into it (*fihi*) some of our spirit, the *hi* referring back to the word *farj* (vagina) earlier in the verse where Mary is said to have remained chaste (that is, "guarded her vagina").

[6] Phyllis Trible's demonstration of the gender nonspecificity of the Biblical Adam in the first creation account might have some bearing on issues in Qur'anic interpretation as well. See P. Trible, *God and the Rhetoric of Sexuality* (Philadelphia: Fortress, 1978); idem, *Texts of Terror: Literary-Feminist Readings of Biblical Narratives* (Philadelphia: Fortress, 1984).

[7]   *wa l-fajr*
     wa layālin *'ashr*
     wa sh-shaf'i wa l-*watr*
     wa l-layli idhā *yasr*
     hal fi dhālika qasamun li dhī ijr

The step-by-step build up in verse length reaches its apogee in the verse that follows, discussing the fate of the people of 'Ād, who, like the people of Thamūd, were destroyed after neglecting the words of their prophet:

     a lam tarā kayfa fa'ala rabbuka bi 'ād?
     "Don't you see what your lord did with 'Ād?"

At this climactic point the end-rhyme shifts to the emotively intense 'Ād, with its long-a in emphatic position at the end of the verse. This shift is strongly reminiscent of the shift in Sura 82:1-6 from staccato, short verses to the long, plaintive refrain *yā ayyuha l-insānu mā gharraka bi rabbika l-karīm* ("Oh, O human being what has deceived you about your generous lord?").

[8] For a summary and discussion of oaths in the Qur'an, see A. Yusuf Ali, *The Holy Quran: Text, Translation, and Commentary* (New York: Hafner, 1946) 2:1784-88.

[9] Fakhr al-Din al-Razi's *Al-Tafsīr al-Kabīr* (The Great Commentary),

vol. 32 (Cairo: Iltizām ʿAbd al-Ra mān Mu ammad, n.d., p.198) is most matter of fact in making the substitution: *mā bi maʿnā man* ("*mā* with the meaning of *man*"). Marmaduke Pickthall, in his popular translation, *The Meaning of the Glorious Coran* (Beirut, dual language edition, n.d., p. 809, renders the last verse as ,"And by Him who made the male and the female," and translates the *mā* similarly in 95:7 and 91:5. Ahmad Ali translates the verse as "And what He created of the male and female." While grammatically possible, this interpretation not only creates the theological difficulty of a male being creating gender, but must create an antecedent for the subject of *khalaqa* (created) that is not only absent from the text but also seems to go against the oath style. See also *al-Quran: a Contemporary Translation* by Ahmed Ali (Princeton, NJ: Princeton University Press, 1988), p. 539.

[10] Other cases are to be found in suras 95:7 and 91:5, 6, 7, the latter of which is especially resonant with the passage in The Night.

[11] The *mā* also resonates with the *ā* sound of *unthā*, and the strong end assonance of *yaghshā* and *tajallā* in the previous verses. This assonance focused on the *ā* sound is the key feature of the sound figures in the Suras of Destiny, The Quaking, and The Qariʿa. We also find in the *wa mā* of *wa mā khalaqa* the "aCā" sequence that was a major sound pattern of Destiny (*wamā, malā, salā*). In each of the three moments, the semantic, emotive, and acoustic energies fall upon units of sound and meaning that are are shaped into sound figures and partial personifications. When it is not dismissed through the substitution of *man* for *mā*), the *mā* in the Sura of Destiny can be heard in its interplay between animate and inanimate, relative and interrogative, an interplay that is intensified through correspondences with other passages.

[12] See Pickthall, *The Meaning of the Glorious Coran*, pp. 808-809. Pickthall appeals to the English literary tradition, in which the sun is personified as male, to reverse the gender of the personification in the Arabic.

[13] Below are some of the sound combinations that, through intratextual and intertextual resonance, become sound figures in certain passages concerning the spirit and the three boundary moments:

fīhā min rūḥinā "some of our spirit into her" (spirit is breathed into Maryam)

rūḥu fīhā "spirit upon her" (spirit descends upon/with the night of destiny)

mā lahā "what is with her?" (asked about the earth in labor and crisis) *hāwiya* "a woman bereft of her child, abyss, falling" (in reference to the *Qāriʿa*)

salāmun hiya "peace she is" (in reference to the night of destiny)

wa ḍuḥāhā "and her brightening" (said about the sun), followed by seven verses with smilar construction (**mā sawwāhā** etc).

wamā, malā, salā, (short a, consonant, long ā patterns from the Sura of Destiny and the Sura of the Night).

[14] R. Bell, *The Qurʾān: Translated, with a Critical Re-Arrangement of the Surahs,* vol. 2 (Edinburgh: T & T Clark, 1937, 1960), p. 669.

Selected Further Resources

The recommendations below are intended for a general audience. A fine overview of Qur'anic scholarship and a full bibliography can be found in Jane Dammen McAuliffe, *Qur'ānic Christians: An Analysis of Classical and Modern Exegesis* (Cambridge University Press, 1991). I have offered detailed recommendations for literature in Arabic and other languages—as well as technical literature on phonetics, linguistics, and other areas—in Michael Sells, "Sound, Spirit, and Gender in Sūrat al-Qadr," *Journal of the American Oriental Society* 11:2 (September, 1990), 101-139; "Sound and Meaning in Sūrat al-Qāri`a," *Arabica* 40 (1993), 403-430.

Qur'an on CD ROM

A major development has in the last decade has brought inexpensive CD ROM versions of the Qur'an to a wide audience. On a single CD, one can find the entire Qur'an, in Arabic, in English transliteration, with several different English translations, and with windows offering discussions of grammar and interpretations by classical commentators. Most important, as the text moves along the screen, the user can listen to the Qur'anic reciter pronouncing the text. Many CD ROMs feature more than one reciter. Among the more popular versions of the Qur'an on CD ROM are:

> *Alim*, includes the Quran with recitation, translation, and other materials.
> *Hoda*, Holy Qur'an and its Stories.
> *Microsystems: The Qur'an on CD-ROM*: Multimedia Presentation of Islam's Holy Book.
> *Sakhr, The Holy Quran*, Sakhr Software.
> *Quran Al Tajweed*-CD.

Cassettes and CDs of Qur'an Recitation

For years recitations of the Qur'an have been popular on cassettes. Now, in industrialized nations CDs are widely available as well. Among the major Qur'anic reciters are Shaykh Maḥmūd al-Ḥusarī and Muḥammad Saddīq al-Minshawī, whose *tartīl* versions of the Qur'an are viewed as authoritative, as well as Shaykh aṭ-Ṭablawī and Shaykh ʿAbd al-Bāsiṭ both of whom who offer both *tartīl* and the more elaborate *tajwīd*. For many of the more famous reciters, recitations of the entire Qurʾan are available in CD or cassette form. Single Suras or sets of shorter Suras are available on individual CDs and cassettes as well.

Among the most popular and respected female Qurʾanic reciters is Hajja Razia bint ʿAbd al-Rahman. Her recitations have been well received at the Malaysian festival featuring women Qurʾan reciters and selections of her recordings are available in the U.S. on cassette. The position of women reciting the Qurʾan in public in Islamic societies resembles that of women ministers in Christianity or women rabbis in Judaism. Depending upon the local culture and version of Islam, women may find themselves encouraged to recite in public or discouraged from public recitation, although all women are encouraged to learn the Qurʾan and to recite it privately.

Qurʾanic Commentary

There is a vast tradition of Quranic commentary. Many of these texts have not been translated into English. In addition to the texts that are found in English on CD ROM, resources in English for this tradition in English include:

Mahmoud Ayoub, *The Qurʾan and Its Interpreters*, vols. 1-2 (Albany: SUNY Press, 1984).

J. M. S. Baljon, *Modern Muslim Koran Interpretation* (Leiden: 1968).

Michael Feener, "Notes toward a History of Qurʾanic Exegesis in Southeast Asia," *Studia Islamica* 5.4 (1988): 47-76.

Helmut Gätje, *The Qurʾan and Its Exegesis: Selected Texts with Classical and Modern Muslim Interpretations* (translated and edited by Alford T. Welch). Oxford: One World Publications, 1996.

J. J. G. Jansen, *The Interpretation of the Koran in Modern Egypt* (Leiden: 1968).

Mustansir Mir, ed., *Tafsīr* 1.1 (January-March 1998). This new journal/newsletter published out of Youngstown State University promises to be a useful resource well into the future.

Journal of Qur'anic Studies is a new publication that will be appearing twice yearly, published through the University of London, Centre of Islamic Studies.

The Commentary on the Quran. Abu Jafar Muhammad b. Jarir al-Tabari (an abridged translation of *Jāmi' al-bayān 'an ta'wīl al-Qur'ān*, with an introduction and notes by J. Cooper (London: New York: Oxford University Press, 1987).

Modern and Comparative Approaches to the Qur'an

For recent general studies, see:

Michael Cook, *The Koran: A Very Short Introduction* (Oxford: Oxford University Press, 2000).

Al-Sayyid Abū al-Qāsim al-Mūsawī al-Khū'i, *The Prolegomena to the Qur'an* (New York: Oxford University Press, 1998). A thorough examination of controversial issues in Quranic studies from a Shi'ite perspective.

Mustansir Mir, "The Qur'an as Literature," *Religion and Literature* 20:1 (1988).

Neal Robinson, *Discovering the Qur'an: A Contemporary Approach to a Veiled Text* (London: SCM Press, 1996).

A wide range of recent scholarship can be found in five collections of essays:

Issa Boullata (ed.), *Literary Structures of Religious Meaning in the Qur'an* (Richmond, Surrey: Curzon Press, 2000).

G. R. Hawting and A. Shareef (eds.) *Approaches to the Qur'an* (London: Routledge, 1993).

A. Rippin (ed.), *Approaches to the History of the Interpretation of the Qur'an* (Oxford: Clarendon Press, 1988).

————— (ed.), *The Qur'an: Style and Contents* (Brooksfield, Vt.: Ashgate, 1999).

————— (ed.), *The Qur'an: Formative Interpretation* (Brooksfield, Vt.: Ashgate, 2000).

For an essay written by a scholar who was not trained in the study of Islam and yet who offers brilliant insights into the language of the Qur'an, see Norman O Brown, "The Apocalypse of Islam," *Social Text* 3:8 (1983-4), 155-171.

For an important comparative discussion see William Graham, *Beyond the Written Word: Oral Aspects of Scripture in the History of Religion* (Cambridge: Cambridge University Press, 1987).

For an analysis of the portrayal of Christians in the Qur'an, along with a clear and full discussion of issues in Qur'anic interpretation and scholarship, see Jane Dammen McAuliffe, *Qur'ānic Christians: An Analysis of Classical and Modern Exegesis* (Cambridge: Cambridge University Press, 1991).

For a thematic discussion of the Qur'an by an influential modern Islamic scholar, see Fazlur Rahman, *Major Themes of the Qur'an* (Minneapolis, MN: Bibliotheca Islamica, 1980).

For a feminist approach to the Qur'an and subsequent traditions, see Fatima Mernissi, *The Veil and the Male Elite: A Feminist Interpretation of Women's Rights in Islam* (translated by Mary Jo Lakeland, Reading, MA: Addison-Wesley, 1991). This book also offers a highly readable and compelling introduction to the life and family of Muhammad, the role of women in the development of Islam, and the stakes behind the controversies surrounding Muhammad and his family.

Excellent work has been done recently on the question women and (and in) the Qur'an. See, for example, Barbara Freyer Stowasser, *Women in the Qur'an: Traditions and Interpretations* (New York: Oxford University Press, 1994); Amina El Azhary Sonbol (ed.), *Women, the Family, and Divorce Laws in Islamic History* (Syracuse: Syracuse University Press, 1996); and Amina Wadud-Muhsin, *Qur'an and Woman: Rereading the Sacred Text from a Woman's Perspective* (Oxford: Oxford University Press, 1999).

For a challenge to Islamic traditions about the Qur'an, see John Wansbrough, *Qur'anic Studies: Sources and Methods of Scriptural Interpretation* (Oxford: Oxford University Press, 1977); and J. Wansbrough, *The Sectarian Milieu* (Oxford: Oxford University Press, 1978). Wansbrough makes difficult reading for the nonspecialist. For an accessible introduction to the issues raised in his work in contrast to the work of Fazlur Rahman, see Andrew Rippin, "Literary Analysis of Qur'an, Tafsir, and Sira: The Methodologies of John Wansbrough and Fazlur Rahman" in Richard Martin (ed), *Approaches to Islam in Religious Studies* (Tucson: University of Arizona Press, 1985), 151-163, 189-202.

For a libration theology approach, see Farid Esack, *Qur'an, Liberation, and Pluralism* (Oxford: One World, 1997).

The Cultural World of Muhammad

For an excellent new study of the legend of Thamūd in Islam and the wider world of myth and symbol in early Arabia, see Jaroslav Stetkevych, *Muhammad and the Golden Bough* (Bloomington: Indiana University Press, 1996).

For the revolution in transport brought about by the new camel saddle and its impact on Arabia, see Richard Bulliet, *The Camel and the Wheel* (Cambridge, MA: Harvard University Press, 1976).

For the earliest major biography (*sīra*) of the prophet Muhammad, see A. Guillaume, *The Life of Muhammad: A Translation of Ibn Ishaq's Sirat Rasul Allah* (Oxford: Oxford University Press, 1987). For another major classical *sīra*, see Ibn Kathir, *The Life of the Prophet* (*Al-Sira al-Nabawiyya*), translated by Trevor Le Gassick, vol 1 of 4 (Reading, UK: Garnet, 1999).

For a modern biography, based on classical tradition, see Martin Lings, *Muhammad: His Life Based on the Earliest Sources* (New York: Inner Traditions, 1983). For the nonspecialist, Lings offers an accessible introduction to the *sīra* literature on Muhammad. For a recent biography based on a non-traditional perspective, see Michael Cook, *Muhammad* (Oxford: Oxford University Press, 1983).

For a particularly accessible and finely balanced portrait of Muhammad's life and times, see Karen Armstrong, *Muhammad: A Biography of the Prophet* (San Francisco: HarperSanFrancisco, 1993).

For an historical study, se F. E. Peters, *Muhammad and the Origins of Islam* (Albany: SUNY Press, 1994).

For pre-Islamic Arabic poetry, see Michael Sells, *Desert Tracings: Six Classical Arabian Odes* (Middletown, CT: Wesleyan University Press, 1989) and Suzanne Pinckey Stetkevych, *The Mute Immortals Speak* (Ithaca, NY: Cornell University Press, 1993).

For a challenge to the premises of traditional Muslim history and the assumptions of Western scholars on the issue of trade routes in Arabia before and at the time of the prophet Muhammad, see Patricia Crone, *Meccan Trade and the Rise of Islam* (Princeton, NJ: Princeton University Press, 1987).

On Qur'anic Recitation

For the major (and highly readable) work in English on the significant in Islamic society of Qur'anic recitation, with deep insight into both the social occasions and the artistic dimensions of the pratice, see Kristina Nelson, *The Art of Reciting the Qur'an* (Austin: University of Texas Press, 1985).

For important new work, see Anna Margaret Gade, *An Envy of Goodness: Learning to Recite the Qur'an in Modern Indonesia* (PhD diss., University of Chicago, 1999).

For an introduction to the rules and practice of *tajwīd*, see Ibrahim H. I. Surty, A Course in "'Ilm al-Tajweed": the Science of Reciting the Quran (Leicester, UK: Islamic Foundation, 1988). The work presupposes some familiarity Arabic.

Those interested in the Qur'an will find that Qur'anic study is still one of the most effective ways of learning Arabic. For those interested in religion, who do not wish to spend years learning the vocabulary of contemporary newspapers or other realms of language, new resources are now available for learning Arabic through the study of the Qur'an. See for example Muhammad Ibrahim Surty, *A Manual of Teaching Arabic Through the Quran* (Elementary).

For further information, see:

Issa J. Boullata, "The Rhetorical Interpretation of the Qur'an: *i'jāz* and Related Topics" in A. Rippin (ed.), *Approaches to the History of the Interpretation of the Qur'an* (Oxford: Clarendon Press, 1988), pp. 139-157.

Frederick Denny, "The Adab of Qur'an Recitation: Text and Context," in Anthony Johns (ed.), *International Congress for the Study of the Qur'an*, Canberra: Australian National University, 1981;

Lamyā' al-Farūqī, "Tartīl al-Qur'ān al-Karīm," in Khurshid Ahmad and Zafar Ansari (eds.), *Islamic Perspectives: Studies in Honor of Mawlānā Sayyid Abul A'lā Mawdūdī* (London: Islamic Foundation U.K. and Jedda, 1979), pp. 105-121;

Frederick Denny, "Exegesis and Recitation: Their Development as Classical Forms of Qur'anic Piety," in Frank E.
Reynolds and T. M. Ludwig (eds.), *Transitions and Transformations in the History of Religions: Essays in Honor of
Joseph M. Kitagawa* (Leiden: Brill, 1980), pp. 91-123;

Frederick Denny and R. L. Taylor (eds.), *The Holy Book in
Comparative Perspective*, (Columbia: University of South
Carolina Press, 1985);

Anne K. Rasmussen, "The Qur'an in Indonesian Daily Life:
The Public Project of Musical Oratory," *Ethnomusicol-
ogy* 45:1 (Winter, 2001): 30-57.

Films and Videocassettes

Khalida Said, *The Power of the Word* (videocassette) 1990, from
the series, *The Arabs: A Living History*. This is an outstanding presentation of expressive language in the Arab world from the Qur'an
and pre-Islamic poetry to the present. The film is centered on the
tragic civil war in Beirut and the efforts of Arab intellectuals to find
resources in expressive language for engaging the tragedy.

Patterns of Beauty (16mm and videocassette, 30 minutes), and
Man and Nature (16mm and videocassette 30 minutes, 1978) These
two films, from the Traditional World of Islam Series, offer stun-
ning visual and aural depictions of Islamic life and society. Patterns
of Beauty is especially useful in presenting the use of Qur'anic calligraphy and other artistic renditions in Islamic art, architecture,
and society. The narrative features quotes from various, usually
unnamed, classical Islamic sources and offers a philosophical, although somewhat triumphalistic, portrayed of Islamic culture.

Reference

A major new resource on the Qur'an is J.D. McAuliffe (ed.), *Ency-
clopaedia of the Qur'an*, the first volume of which is now under-
way (Leiden: Brill, 1999 —).

The two editions of the *Encyclopedia of Islam* (Leiden: Brill,
1913) and (Leiden: Brill, 1960) also contain important reference
information. Both editions are widely available in the reference
rooms of university and major public libraries.

See also Hanna E. Kassis, *A Concordance of the Qur'an* (Berkeley: University of California Press, 1983), and Mustansir Mir, *Dictionary of Qur'anic Terms and Concepts* (New York: Garland, 1987).

English Renditions of the Qur'an:
The Qur'an: Translated, With a Critical Rearrangement of the Surahs, translated by Richard Bell (Edinburgh: T. & T. Clark, 1939. From the point of view of literary style and accuracy, this is one of the finer English renditions of the Qur'an. It is difficult to read, however, because Bell's "critical rearrangement" of the Suras chops them up according to the self-confident views of the translator on the chronology of the revelations to Muhammad. Still this work is one of the most important sources in English and well worth consulting even by those who are not interested in Bell's rearrangement project. It is especially valuable for its close adherence to the Qur'anic cadence and verbal rhythm.

The Koran Interpreted, by Arthur J. Arberry (London: Allen & Unwin; New York: Macmillan, 1955).

The Meaning of the Glorious Koran: An Explanatory Translation, translated by Marmaduke Pickthall (London: Knopf, 1930). This volume is frequently available in bilingual, facing-page version.

The Koran, translated by N.J. Dawood (New York: Penguin Books, 1972), and *The Koran*, translated by N.J. Dawood (New York: Penguin Books, 1990). In the first edition, Dawood rearranged the Qur'an according to what is believed about its chronological order, beginning with some of the early Meccan Suras that appear at the end of the standard written text. In the new edition, the traditional arrangement of the Suras is used.

Al-Qur'ān: A Contemporary Translation, translated by Ahmed Ali (Princeton, NJ: Princeton University Press, 1988). This translation, in a bilingual facing-page presentation, offers a more natural language than the neo-Victorian language of Arberry or the extremely literal and stiff language of Pickthall.

The Holy Quran. Text, Translation, and Commentary by Abdullah Yusuf Ali (New York: Hafner Publishing, 1946). This is a highly respected work and is considered a standard English rendition by many Muslims.

The Qur'an, translation and commentary by T. B. Irving (Brattleboro, VT: Amana Books, 1988). This version like Ahmad Ali's, works for a natural idiom—in this case with an American expressive style.

The Awesome News, Interpretation of Juz' 'Amma—The Last Part of the Qur'an, by Mahmoud M. Ayoub (World Call Society, second edition, 1997). The translation and commentary by Ayoub are excellent and provide a fine study of the Qur'anic passages examined above.

The Message of the Qur'an, translated by Muhammad Asad (Chicago: Kazi Publications, 1992).

The Essential Koran, translated by Thomas Cleary (San Francisco: Harper, 1994).

Camille Adams Helminski, *The Light of Dawn: a Daybook of Verses from the Holy Qur'an* (Putney, VT: Threshold Books, 1998).

COMPACT DISC RECORDING
The Call to Prayer and Six Suras
1 The Opening (al-fatiha), 82 The Tearing (al-infitar), 91 The Sun (ash-shams), 97 Destiny (al-qadr), 99 The Earthquake (al-zalzala), 101 The Calamity (al-qari'a)

For translations, transliterations, and sound cues to these tracks, see pages 150-180.

Call to Prayer (adhan)
| Track 1 | By Mustafa Ozcan Gunesdogdu | (Sunni Adhan) |

Muhammad Khalil al-Husari (Murattal)
Track 2	Surat al-Fatiha	(Sura 1)
Track 3	Surat al-Infitar	(Sura 82)
Track 4	Surat ash-Shams	(Sura 91)
Track 5	Surat al-Qadr	(Sura 97)
Track 6	Surat az-Zalzala	(Sura 99)
Track 7	Surat al-Qari'a	(Sura 101)

Hajjah Maria Ulfa (Murattal)
Track 8	Surat al-Infitar	(Sura 82)
Track 9	Surat ash-Shams	(Sura 91)
Track 10	Surat al-Qadr	(Sura 97)
Track 11	Surat az-Zalzala	(Sura 99)
Track 12	Surat al-Qari'a	(Sura 101)

Hajjah Maria Ulfa (Mujawwad)
Track 13	Surat al-Qadr	(Sura 97)
Track 14	Surat az-Zalzala	(Sura 99)
Track 15	Surat al-Qari'a	(Sura 101)

'Abd al-Basit 'Abd al-Samad
Track 16	Surat al-Infitar	(Sura 82)
Track 17	Surat ash-Shams	(Sura 91)
Track 18	Surat al-Qadr	(Sura 97)
Track 19	Surat az-Zalzala	(Sura 99)
Track 20	Surat al-Qari'a	(Sura 101)

217

Imam Zijad Delic

| Track 21 | Surat al-Qari'a | (Sura 101) |
| Track 22 | Surat az-Zalzala | (Sura 99) |

Muhammad Siddiq al-Minshawi (Murattal)

Track 23	Surat al-Fatiha	(Sura 1)
Track 24	Surat al-Infitar	(Sura 82)
Track 25	Surat ash-Shams	(Sura 91)
Track 26	Surat al-Qadr	(Sura 97)
Track 27	Surat az-Zalzala	(Sura 99)
Track 28	Surat al-Qari'a	(Sura 101)

Seemi Bushra Ghazi

Track 29	Surat al-Qadr (two versions)	(Sura 97)
Track 30	Surat az-Zalzala	(Sura 99)
Track 31	Surat al-Qari'a	(Sura 101)

Call to Prayer (adhan)

| Track 32 | By Amir Koushkani | (Shi'i Adhan) |

Imam Bilal Hyde

| Track 33 | Live Recitation of Surat al-Fatiha | (Sura 1) |

BIOGRAPHIES OF QURANIC RECITERS

Mustafa Ozcan Gunesdogdu is one of the most distinguished recent representatives of the Turkish tradition of Qur'an recitation and *adhān*. His recitations have received international recognition and prizes at Qur'an recitation festivals.

Muhammad Khalil al-Husari was for many years the acknowledged master of the *murattal* style of recitation. Husari combined scholarship and artistry with restraint in use of melodic effects. The result is a recitation that is at once simple and profound.

Hajjah Maria Ulfah, winner of two Indonesian national Qur'an recitation contests, is internationally recognized as one of the world's master reciters and teachers of recitation. She is Manager of the Central Institute for the Development of Quranic Recitation and Lecturer at the Institute for the Study of the Qur'an and at the National Islamic University in Indonesia.

'Abd al-Basit 'Abd as-Samad exemplified the Egyptian popular reciter. In his recordings, now circulating throughout the Islamic world, he combines a clear and high-register articulation with a sense of dramatic urgency.

Imam Zijad Delic received his advanced studies in Sarajevo and Islamabad. He worked with the Islamic community in Donji Vakuf, Bosnia and among Bosnians in exile, and is now Imam of the Richmond, Vancouver mosque. He is currently recording an album of *anāshīd* (devotional songs) in Bosnian and Arabic.

Muhammad Siddiq al-Minshawi, another Egyptian reciter, combined the classical restraint and contemplative quality of Husari's recitation with a particularly poignant example of *taḥzīn*, the evocation and expression of sadness as a Qur'anic meditation.

Seemi Bushra Ghazi represents the cultivation of recitation by the gifted non-professional. She lives in Vancouver, British Columbia and is known for her participation in a variety of Islamic cultural events and Sufi devotional chants.

Amir Koushkani was trained in classical Persian music under Master Darioush Peerniakhan. He has pursued his art in Iran and internationally and currently resides in Vancouver, British Columbia. Among his recordings is an album of Persian Sufi poetry set to music in collaboration with Houman Pourmehdi entitled *Quest* (Vancouver: Songlines Recordings, 1998).

Imam Bilal Hyde was trained in religious studies at McGill University and the University of California, Berkeley and in traditional Islamic studies in Mecca, Medina, Ethiopia, The Sudan, and Egypt. He serves as Muslim chaplain in the California State Prison system, teaches Qur'anic recitation and interpretation, serves as Imam for the Mevlevi, Chisti, and Jerrahi Sufi Orders, and participates in ecumenical gatherings, particularly through San Francisco's Grace Cathedral.